Data Driven Differentiation

in the **Standards-Based Classroom**

Gayle H. Gregory · Lin Kuzmich

CORWIN PRESS
A Sage Publications Company
Thousand Oaks, California

For information:

Corwin Press
A Sage Publications Company
2455 Teller Road
Thousand Oaks, California 91320
www.corwinpress.com

Sage Publications Ltd.
1 Oliver's Yard
55 City Road
London EC1Y 1SP
United Kingdom

Sage Publications India Pvt. Ltd.
B-42, Panchsheel Enclave
Post Box 4109
New Delhi 110 017 India

Printed in the United States of America

Library of Congress Cataloging-in-Publication Data

Gregory, Gayle.
Data driven differentiation in the standards-based classroom/Gayle H. Gregory,
Lin Kuzmich.
    p. cm.
Includes bibliographical references and index.
ISBN 0–7619–3157–0 (cloth)—ISBN 0–7619–3158–9 (paper)
    1. Individualized instruction. 2. Education—Standards. 3. Curriculum planning.
4. Educational tests and measurements. I. Kuzmich, Lin. II. Title. LB1031.G733 2004
371.39′4—dc22
                                    2003024016

04   05   06   07   10   9   8   7   6   5   4   3

Acquisitions Editor:	Faye Zucker
Editorial Assistant:	Stacy Wagner
Production Editor:	Melanie Birdsall
Copy Editor:	Jacqueline Tasch
Typesetter:	C&M Digitals (P) Ltd.
Proofreader:	Scott Oney
Indexer:	Kathy Paparchontis
Cover Designer:	Tracy E. Miller
Graphic Designer:	Lisa Miller

Data Driven Differentiation
in the Standards-Based Classroom

Contents

Preface

When we began teaching, back when the Earth was cooling, there were no standards. We were given a piece of paper with a few math facts and another with social studies topics relating to the neighborhood for Gayle's Grade 3/4 classroom and for Lin's PreK to 12 reading and special education students. We had limited training as to what and how we were to teach. Basically, we built the road as we traveled through the curriculum, more "gosh and by golly" than intentional.

We wanted to do the best for our students, but there were few guidelines, and our lack of experience left us little to draw on. Gayle realized that even though she had won the top teaching award out of 875 graduates at her university, in the classroom, she didn't even know what she didn't know. Lin struggled to find assessments and to figure out how to meet the needs of struggling adolescents, many of whom had initial versions of Individualized Education Plans. Even with some information about her students, Lin was not really certain what the objectives were for other classes. At that time, the targets for learning were inconsistent or just not in place at all. The standards and benchmarks available to us now provide welcome guidelines to help teachers know where they are going and how to judge success, both for themselves and for their students.

Intuitively, we did our best to integrate learning around themes, as that seemed to be a way to engage students and tie the curriculum together. However, instructional units were designed not around standards (as we had none) but rather around neat learning activities. We also lacked assessment strategies so we didn't always know what students knew or could do. So we planned great units of study, but the wrong students came. They were in different places than we thought they might be, and they had different interests, capabilities, and intelligences. Or we had a great lesson plan, but it just didn't work for some of our students. Gayle didn't have enough tools and information about learning in her repertoire to do much more than "say it louder and slower" one more time when students had difficulty, but that method often didn't work. Of course, whether it worked was not really an issue then because there was really little accountability at that time. Teachers taught, and the students' job was to learn. Lin's first experience with other content-area teachers and their reactions to her students was disappointing. It was hard for content-trained teachers to account for differences in reading and writing skills. We simply had not been taught those strategies. Teachers really had little inclination and few resources to persevere until *all* students learned.

Thankfully, we had a group of committed, seasoned teachers at hand in those first schools who were generous and encouraging and who shared materials and strategies with us. Today, we are fortunate to have both standards that clearly show us the target and a set of solidly research-based instructional techniques and assessment tools to facilitate learning for a diverse group of learners. Gayle's daughter and son-in-law are teachers at the beginning of their careers, and she has watched with interest as they continue to evolve in their new roles. They have the advantage of "beginning with the end in mind," with standards to guide their thinking and planning. Their knowledge base and skill development in teaching are ever expanding in relation to the diverse group of students they serve. Special education students, students with emotional and behavioral disorders, students learning English as a second language, and multiple other groups of students are in their classrooms, and they are constantly trying to respond to the complexity of the mix with varying approaches to teaching and learning. Standardized tests are also a reality for them and cannot be ignored. They see the stress this testing creates for students and parents, but they also know that there are so many other worthwhile facets of the assessment process that inform them about students and their progress.

As an assistant superintendent, Lin faces the challenge of continual updates about the latest regulations, rules, and legislation affecting schools. Teachers, too, face new pressures and dilemmas as they try to meet the needs of diverse students. Lin's talented staff are far more prepared today to meet current challenges, yet even with all the excellent training available to them, they continue to have questions. In Lin's district, hardworking teachers, committed administrators, and a supportive board of education are all trying to make the right choices for students. While we know so much more about learning, questions still remain about where and how to focus our precious time with students and still meet the high criteria for accountability. With such limited time and resources, how can staff make the best choices for students with very different needs and styles?

This book is our attempt to help all teachers and administrators make sense of planning from standards, differentiating learning for the diversity in their classrooms, and using the data that they collect from their students. We would have been so grateful all those years ago to know what we know now. It is an exciting time to be in education with all that we have discovered and researched in the last 30 years. Teaching truly is an art and a science. We believe the creativity of great teachers mixed with the knowledge and skills we now have make our profession a challenging and exciting one both for teachers and for students.

ACKNOWLEDGMENTS

This book was written by two educators who have spent many years in schools "trying to get it right." Gayle Gregory and Lin Kuzmich both are teachers and practitioners at heart and have worked with teachers and students over the years in a variety of roles and grade levels. Our interest in this topic is an evolving quest to help teachers work with standards to plan assessment, curriculum, instruction, and learning, standards that address the diversity in classrooms today so that all children may learn to their potential.

We would like to acknowledge all those other talented and committed educators who have challenged our thinking and helped clarify our ideas based on sound research and practice.

We have been enlightened and influenced by great thinkers, including Howard Gardner, Robert Sternberg, Daniel Goleman, Art Costa, Bob Garmstom, Pat Wolfe, Robert Sylwester, Barbara Givens, David Sousa, Tony Gregorc, Carol Rolheiser, Bob Marzano, Jay McTighe, Carol Ann Tomlinson, Pam Robbins, Heidi Hayes Jacob, Grant Wiggins, Richard Stiggins, Doug Reeves, Linda Elder, and Richard Paul.

We wish to thank Faye Zucker for her support, advice, patience, encouragement, and sense of humor during the writing process. Our thanks also go to Stacy Wagner and Jacqueline Tasch for their diligence during editing and reviewing and to our production editor, Melanie Birdsall.

Finally, we extend our gratitude to our husbands, Joe and Steve, and to our children for their patience and understanding about the time this venture took from "family hour." We could not accomplish anything worthwhile without their love and support.

It is our hope and desire that this book will be a helpful, insightful addition to the libraries of teachers, administrators, and other educators and an integral part of their planning and thinking as they design learning for all children so that all may learn and reach their potential.

Corwin Press and the authors extend their thanks to the following reviewers for their contributions to this volume:

Kathleen Chamberlain, Ph.D., Lycoming College, Williamsport, PA

Steve Hutton, Elementary School Principal, Villa Hills, KY

Mildred Murray-Ward, Ph.D., California Lutheran University, Thousand Oaks, CA

Maria Elena Reyes, Ph.D., University of Alaska, Fairbanks, AK

About the Authors

 **Gayle H. Gregory** has been a teacher in elementary, middle, and secondary schools. For many years, she taught in schools with extended periods of instructional time (block schedules). She has had extensive districtwide experience as a curriculum consultant and staff development coordinator. Most recently, she was course director at York University for the Faculty of Education, teaching in the teacher education program. She now consults internationally (Europe, Asia, North and South America, Australia) with teachers, administrators, and staff developers in the areas of managing change, differentiated instruction, brain-compatible learning, block scheduling, emotional intelligence, instructional and assessment practices, cooperative group learning, presentation skills, renewal of secondary schools, enhancing teacher quality, coaching and mentoring, and facilitating large scale change.

Gayle is affiliated with many organizations, including the Association for Supervision and Curriculum Development and the National Staff Development Council. She is the author of *Differentiated Instructional Strategies in Practice: Training, Implementation, and Supervision* and the coauthor of *Designing Brain-Compatible Learning; Thinking Inside the Block Schedule: Strategies for Teaching in Extended Periods of Time;* and *Differentiated Instructional Stategies: One Size Doesn't Fit All.* She has been featured in *Video Journal of Education*'s best-selling elementary and secondary videos, *Differentiating Instruction to Meet the Needs of All Learners.*

Gayle is committed to lifelong learning and professional growth for herself and others. She may be contacted by e-mail at gregorygayle@netscape.net. Her Web site is www3.sympatico.ca/gayle.gregory.

Lin Kuzmich is the assistant superintendent for Thompson School District in Loveland, Colorado, where she has also served as executive director of instruction, as director of professional development, and for nine years as a principal. Before joining the Loveland District, Lin was a classroom teacher. She taught special education and reading PreK-12, high school reading, and middle school language arts, and she was also an elementary school classroom teacher, earning the Teacher of the Year Award for Denver Public Schools in 1979.

For the past 10 years Lin has been involved in professional development, teaching classes at several universities, providing training for agencies and school districts throughout the United States, and authoring journal articles and government and regional publications. Her recent work has focused on data driven instruction, standards-based education, supervision and evaluation of teachers, and data driven school improvement planning. Lin works extensively with administrators and teacher leaders who want to create an environment for student achievement and growth.

Lin may be contacted through Thompson School District in Loveland, Colorado.

Introduction

Differentiating With Data for Student Growth and Achievement

WHAT IS OUR TARGET?

Today, the reality for teachers has shifted dramatically from a decade ago. No longer can we go into classrooms and "spray and pray," hoping students will succeed. We are being held accountable for all learners, not only those who learn in spite of us but also those who learn because of us.

The 21st-century learner differs immensely from learners even a generation ago. Today's students look at typewriters, audiotapes, and rotary dial telephones as antiques that belong in a museum. They can't imagine a world where communication and access to information isn't achieved in a nanosecond with technology that should be commonplace to them. Thus to use methods and techniques from the last century doesn't connect to the reality of the learners' world today. These students live in a cyber-tech environment where pencil and paper often have little appeal and where novelty or relevance and meaning are a great need when it comes to ideas and information.

The world around learners demands new and different competencies if they are to succeed in the future. Thornburg (2002) reminds us that the world is in a constant state of flux. We continue to administer standardized tests with content that may be irrelevant in the world where students live. Beyond the test is the reality of the workplace and living a full and successful life in an ever changing environment. Without a crystal ball, teachers go forth courageously trying to prepare learners for a world whose shape is uncertain, a world that we may never see ourselves.

"According to Robert Reich (1992), the quality jobs of the future will belong to 'symbolic analysts'—people who solve, identify, and broker problems by manipulating images" (Thornburg, 2002, p. 32). Reich's basic skills include abstraction, system thinking, experimentation, and collaboration.

WHY DIFFERENTIATE?

No longer is it an option to let students fall "through the cracks." We recognize that they learn because of us and the learning opportunities that we provide for the diverse learners that we have in classrooms today. As educators (and parents), we know that learners differ in many ways. Whether it is in appearance, learning style, multiple intelligence, prior experience, personal preference, or social/emotional development, students differ. Around the world, teachers are rising to the challenge of meeting the needs of those diverse learners while keeping the integrity of targeted standards. We want not to lower the bar but indeed to raise the level of success and to increase growth for all students.

Thus, differentiating instruction to meet those diverse learners is a philosophy that teachers embrace, and there are ways to differentiate learning processes that are appropriate at different times in different situations with different learners. Students don't all learn the same thing on the same day in the same way. The dilemma for us as educators is to know the students well enough and to have a repertoire that can be used selectively and strategically based on the standards, the content, and the learners' needs. Knowing when, why, and how is the science of teaching. The art of teaching is the creativity that teachers use to include learners in the learning process based on their needs. The key to reaching targeted standards is planning for growth so that each learner may succeed to the best of his or her ability.

In this book, we explore ways of planning that consider

- Targeted standards
- Data about students and their knowledge, skills (pre-assessment, formative or ongoing, and summative), and ability to think diagnostically

- Information about students as individuals (learning styles, multiple intelligence, interests, preferences, developmental needs: social, emotional, physical)
- Unit planning (backward design)
- Lesson planning (chunking the learning to facilitate daily student engagement and rehearsal)

THEATERS OF THE MIND: LEARNING SYSTEMS AND THE BRAIN

What do we know about learning and student growth? In recent years, we have learned a lot about how the brain is organized and functions, and what we have learned raises questions for us as teachers.

According to Ornstein (1986), the brain is a complex biological organ with several systems embedded in its structures:

> Stuck side by side, inside the skin, inside the skull, are several special purpose, separate, and specific small minds. . . . The particular collection of talents, abilities, and capacities that each person possesses depends partly on birth and partly on experience. Our illusion is that each of us is somehow unified, with a single coherent purpose and action. . . . We are not a single person. We are many. . . . All of these general components of the mind can act independently of each other, [and] they may well have different priorities. (pp. 8–9)

These functions are not processed consciously but occur automatically. Restak (1994) identifies five systems that interact constantly as we receive, process, and interpret information. It is like a multiplex theater that never closes, according to Barbara Given (2002), where several movies are playing at the same time. The five systems are as follows:

- Emotional learning system
- Social learning system
- Physical learning system
- Cognitive learning system
- Reflective learning system (see Figure 0.1)

The emotional, social, and physical systems are greedy for attention and will not allow the cognitive and reflective systems to function at optimal efficiency if their needs are not met.

Figure 0.1 Five Theaters of the Mind

Emotional	Social	Cognitive	Physical	Reflective
• Climate • *Emotional safety* • Relevancy • Meaning	• Inclusion • Respect • Enjoy others • Interaction • Interpersonal • Sharing • Authentic situations • Tolerance	• Academic skill development • Prior and new learning connected • Seeks patterns, concepts, themes • Likes to see wholes and parts	• Requires active involvement • Enjoys challenging tasks that encourage practice • Skills are a major part of this system	• Personal reflection on one's own learning styles • Reflects on successes, failures, changes needed • Metacognition of one's own strengths and preferences

SOURCE: Adapted from Barbara Given, 2002.

Emotional Learning System

It has long been known that negative emotions and social interactions can inhibit academic progress (Rozman, 1998). Students will spend an inordinate amount of attention and energy protecting themselves from ridicule and rejection rather than learning new knowledge and skills.

Researchers tell us that we need emotional nourishment from birth (Kessler, 2000; Palmer, 1993). Lack of it affects us profoundly. Endorphins and norepinephrine (the feel-good neurotransmitters released in the brain during positive experiences) influence positive emotions and support learning, along with good health and success in life (Pert, 1993). Emotions are both innate and acquired. Surprisingly, peers and siblings have much more impact on learned emotions (45%) than do parents (5%), according to Harris (1998).

When emotional needs such as love and acceptance are met, the brain produces serotonin (a feel-good neurotransmitter). When emotional needs are not met, young people often turn to drugs that obliterate the negative feelings of hunger, fatigue, and depression. A natural high can result through connectedness and meaningful interactions, interesting learning materials, and attention to students' personal needs and goals. Csikszentmihalyi (1990) refers to the "state of flow" where all systems are focused and challenge is matched to skill level. In this state, all systems are go and work together toward optimal learning.

The emotional system flourishes in classrooms and schools

- Where educators and students believe students can learn and be successful
- Where students' hopes and dreams are recognized
- Where teachers make learning relevant to students' lives
- Where teachers provide multiple ways for students to express themselves
- Where teachers continue to challenge students
- Where the climate nurtures rather than represses

Social Learning System

From birth, we begin to form relationships with others and our environment to better understand ourselves. There are two social subsystems. One system in place at birth relates to dyadic relationships. The other evolves and deals with group relationships (Harris, 1998). The extent to which we feel part of a group influences our behavior in and out of school. All of us prefer to interact with those whose presence increases the brain's feel-good neurotransmitter brain levels, resulting from feelings of comfort, trust, respect, and affection (Panksepp, 1998). Yet, often in classrooms, there is no opportunity to develop social interactions that promote trust and connections. We naturally tend to participate in groups so that we feel a kinship that is fostered by group norms and values (Wright, 1994).

A skillful, insightful teacher can capitalize on this knowledge by creating a classroom climate that

- Includes all learners
- Honors their hopes and aspirations
- Provides an enriched environment for authentic learning (Given, 2002)

Physical Learning System

The physical learning system involves active problem-solving challenges. It is often the system that is not used enough in classrooms, even though we know that gifted students (Milgram, Dunn, & Price, 1993) and underachievers (Dunn, 1990) have a preference for active, tactile, and kinesthetic involvement when learning new material.

Those of us who have found learners in our classrooms who need to have the physical learning system in the forefront have realized that if we ignore this system, the learners will find a way to move to satisfy their needs regardless of our plans. Their movement might have nothing to do with the knowledge or skills that have been targeted for learning. So it begs the question: Do we build in opportunities for hands-on, active learning, or do we let students find a way of their own to use physical systems, a way that may be counterproductive to the learning?

Cognitive Learning System

This is the system that we focus on most often in the classroom, and rightly so as we want students to succeed in learning new knowledge and skills. The cognitive system deals with consciousness, language development, focused attention, and memory. This system also relies on the senses for processing information. Thus, good teachers facilitate learning by providing information in a novel way, stimulating the visual, auditory, and tactile senses as well as taste and smell, if appropriate. However, as previously noted, the emotional, social, and physical systems seem more greedy for attention, and if their needs are not attended to, students will not be comfortable enough to learn. If all systems are go, students tend to learn with more ease and with greater retention.

Reflective Learning System

Dr. Art Costa has been known to say that intelligent people "know what to do when they don't know what to do." People learn from experience only if they reflect on the experience.

This intelligence includes "thinking strategies, positive attitudes toward investing oneself in good thinking, and metacognition—awareness and management of one's own mind" Perkins, 1995, p. 234). Damasio (1999) notes that the reflective system involves the interdependence of memory systems, communication systems, reason, attention, emotion, social awareness, physical experiences, and sensory modalities.

The reflective system allows us to

- Analyze situations
- Examine and react
- Make plans
- Guide behaviors toward goals

This is the system that, in the rush to cover the curriculum, is often left out of the learning process in the classroom. However, the skills of ongoing reflection and self-examination are key to evolving the self. These metacognitive skills enable students to form a clear image of self and to develop the reflective strategies that lead to self-directed learning and success in life.

LEARNING SYSTEMS AND STUDENT GROWTH

In each chapter of this book, we will look at the interaction of these learning systems and their impact on the learning process. We will acknowledge that every brain is unique and that how smart we are is not as important as how we are smart. Being cognizant of learning styles and preferences is another lens through which we know our learners and respond to their interests and needs. This knowledge is imperative for planning purposes and identification of the hook each learner needs to become engaged with the learning.

We have also acquired research about instructional best practices that show great promise for student achievement. In *Classroom Instruction That Works,* Marzano, Pickering, and Pollack (2001) propose research on nine essential strategies and provide a field book full of examples of these strategies in a variety of subject areas. These nine strategies have a profound impact on student learning, as much as 22 to 45 percentile gains in student achievement. Figure 0.2 shows the nine essential strategies and their percentile gains (Marzano et al., 2001).

If we are going to differentiate instruction for students, it probably would be best to include the best instructional strategies that we have available to us so that the chances of student learning and achievement are greater. In this book, we will endeavor to help teachers plan to use brain research as well as the pedagogical best practices to increase student engagement and learning with a diverse population.

Figure 0.2 Nine Essential Teaching Strategies and Associated Percentile Gains in Student Achievement

Recognizing similarities and differences, using metaphors and analogies	45
Summarizing and note taking	37
Reinforcing effort and providing recognition	29
Homework and practice	28
Nonlinguistic representations	27
Cooperative learning	27
Setting objectives and providing feedback	23
Generating and testing hypotheses	23
Questions, cues, and advance organizers	22

SOURCE: Marzano et al., 2001.

CONNECTING DATA TO LEARNING

Where is the connection between data and learning? Many teachers teach much the way they were taught. They ask the following questions:

- What is the next chapter in the book?
- How much content do I need to cover?
- How will I teach this skill or content?

We call this commonly used style "teach, test, and hope for the best."

Standards-based education facilitated the beginnings of a shift from these teacher-centered questions to a greater focus on student learning. The new questions are the following:

- What should my students know and be able to do?
- How will I know they "get it"?
- What activity might be motivating for students?
- What learning processes will I offer or facilitate?
- What will I do if that doesn't work?

These questions are an excellent start. However, we may need to pose other questions since the target for success is changing. It is not enough to demonstrate standards; now we must pose questions that help us focus on student growth.

Research-Based Instructional Strategies

Many fine educators respond to this louder call for student growth with an increased focus on strategies. Excellent research, the kind with large effect sizes and replication of results, is summarized in Marzano et al. (2001). Doug Reeves (2000) also reminds us that it's unrealistic to think that teachers or any professional would come into the profession with all the knowledge and skills necessary to do the job. Learning is a continuous lifelong process as new information and strategies are identified that should be added to our repertoire.

As we retool for this next challenge, a focus only on varying the research-based strategies may not produce the results we want for our students. We must also retool our metacognition about teaching and learning to include the relationship of these strategies to what we know about the achievement levels of our students.

Sally L. has been teaching for twenty-two years in middle or junior high schools. She is frequently puzzled by phenomena she has noticed over the years. Even when she uses a variety of strategies and materials, not all of her students perform well on assessments, and some rarely demonstrate the ability to generalize that learning across curricula or time.

Sally has learned about performance assessment design and standards over the last ten years. Before that, she carefully studied objectives and elements of instruction. Sally is the type of teacher whom principals value. She frequently mentors new teachers and considers herself a lifelong learner. Sally has been told that student growth is important, as if she didn't know that already. Current accountability practices in her district leave Sally frustrated rather than empowered. How can she get more students to perform and think at deeper levels about the standards she is teaching?

Sally is not alone. Then again, she may be asking the wrong questions. Schools often use high-stakes data these days to plan for school improvement and governmental accountability. Could we apply some of the best of these practices to the classroom? Could we begin to make decisions involving data about what and how we teach and how students learn?

Standards-Based and Data Driven Instructional Strategies

Standards-based and data driven decision making in the classroom is about connecting what we know about students and what we want them to learn in relation to the standards with the best possible strategy for success. We need to know where and how students are performing when they walk into our classrooms. Then, using the standards-based final assessment as our target, we will ask a different set of questions:

- What do we know about students' readiness, ability, and interests in relationship to the standards and benchmarks?
- What thinking, skills, products, and processes will they need to demonstrate on the final assessment?
- What don't I know about their skills and thinking, strengths, and preferences?
- How will I know if students are making progress along the way, before they attempt the final assessment?

Sally may find that answering these questions helps more students achieve at proficient levels in a reasonable amount of time. If Sally can systematically plan student learning to close the gap between what students will need to do and know and what they can accomplish now, her instruction and therefore the learning will result in the growth of more students.

USING CLASSROOM DATA TO PLAN DIFFERENTIATED INSTRUCTIONAL STRATEGIES

Beware of the learning gap—you may fall into it. High-stakes data gives us only one piece of evidence about student learning. Well-designed classroom data collection and analysis, the everyday information a teacher collects, form the backbone of student growth. Collecting the right data and then understanding the data feels like a monumental task to most teachers. We hope to give you insights and practical strategies for designing pre-assessments, formative assessments, and final assessments that give you useful data. We also want to help you craft the diagnostic thinking to tie what you know about students to how you choose to grow their skills.

Diagnostic Thinking

Effective use of classroom data increases the probability that more students will demonstrate proficient and higher levels of performance. When to collect that data and how to ensure quality assessment practices are essential components in reaching our desired target (Stiggins, 1997).

Diagnostic thinking involves the understanding of cause and effect on student learning.

- If I do this or if students do this, what effect can I reasonably expect?
- If I know this about my learners, what strategies, materials, grouping, and amount of time may result in the greatest learning?
- Are my expectations for students appropriate given the standards I want them to demonstrate?
- What type of learners may be successful using which type of learning practice?

While this type of planning, instruction, and learning takes some time-consuming, up-front work, it has numerous long-term benefits. Data driven decision making helps teachers maximize the limited time they have with students. Given the improved accuracy of instruction from this type of planning, teachers can reduce the amount of repetition and review in the curriculum.

TARGETING GROWTH FOR ALL STUDENTS

Accurate instruction also increases the chances that more students will reach the target. That is, after all, the bottom line. If our target is the growth of all students, how do we get there? The gap between what feels good in teaching and what works, and for which students it works, is vast. We hope this book closes that decision-making gap for you. In Figure 0.3 we offer you an outline of the elements in each chapter of this book that will help you use data to ensure student growth and achievement.

Figure 0.3 Differentiating With Data for Student Growth and Achievement

Data to Create Climate	Data to Know the Learner	Assessment Data	Curriculum Design	Adjustable Assignments	Instructional Strategies
Building connections • Risk taking • Theaters of the mind • Resilience • Nurture Foster and sustain growth • Feedback • Reflective learning • Rituals • Respect • Cultural history • States of mind • Celebration • Higher level thinking	Learning styles • Strengths • Needs • Attitudes • Preferences Eight multiple intelligences Intelligent behavior • Persistence • Listening • Metacognition • Flexibility • Accuracy and precision • Posing questions and problems • Experience and new application • Sensory • Creativity • Efficacy	Diagnostic thinking • Pre-assessment • Formative assessment • Formal versus informal data collection • Performance assessments Analyze formative data • Grouping • Selecting differentiation strategies • Critical thinking The role of other forms of assessment • Using summative data • Self-assessment	Curriculum mapping • Standards-based • Focus and target • Expectations Unit planning • Standards • Benchmarks or objectives • Key concepts • Skills • Critical questions • The role of critical thinking • Relevance • Final assessment • Rubric • Pre-assessment • Chunking a unit • Transition points	TAPS • Total group • Alone • Pairs • Small group Adjustable grids • Compacting • Adjusting for competency • Content and materials • Communication and technology • Multiple intelligences • Readiness • Interest and choice • Process and rehearsal	Best practices strategies for • Sensory memory • Short-term memory • Long-term memory Research-based strategies • Inductive thinking • Note taking and summarizing • Homework • Nonlinguistic representations • Cooperative group learning Unit lesson planning

Collecting Data to Create a Positive Classroom Climate   1

POSITIVE CLASSROOM CONNECTIONS

Why are connections essential? The essence of human interaction is social, based on relationships. To create a fertile soil for learning, teachers and students must make daily and positive connections. Without connections, the definition of being at-risk becomes a reality.

Interviewing students in an alternative high school or a drop-out prevention program produces a litany of connections "gone bad" at critical junctures in students' lives. Students frequently report that they could go days without an adult who smiled or personally interacted with them. Hiding at school became an art form with these students. In contrast, on a recent visit to a secondary school in Colorado, an administrator noted the concerted effort of staff there to uncover and rid the school of "hiding opportunities."

To foster connections, each of the more than 1,100 students in the Colorado school was listed on a series of large charts. Staff members marked off students with whom they had frequent (daily was preferred) and personal contact. The staff then walked among the charts, and each teacher, administrator, and support member put his or her name next to two or three of the 137 students whom the data showed were getting no regular contact. The next quarter, staff reported a marked decline in both discipline issues and the drop-out rate and an increase in attendance. While this method of analysis and data use is not new, the results tend to be well worth the time and effort of staff. Students are always worth time and effort, especially when we establish connections.

When we reviewed the "Five Theaters of the Mind" model (see Figure 0.1), we learned that the emotional, social, and physical systems of the mind are greedy for attention and will not allow the cognitive and reflective systems to function at optimal efficiency if their needs are not met. Understanding these "theaters" is one way to see how connections affect learning and, therefore, why collecting data and using it to make differentiated changes in learning environments is essential.

Caring and Support

Rachael Kessler (2000) describes deep connection as one of seven gateways to the "soul of education":

> The yearning for deep connection describes a quality of relationship that is profoundly caring, is resonant with meaning, and involves feelings of belonging, or of being truly seen and known. (p. 17)

Students need opportunities to receive care and support from adults to form deep connections. They also need developmentally appropriate opportunities for steadily increasing autonomy and choice. Competent adults who demonstrate caring and appropriate supervision are key components in developing students' self-confidence, which results in acceptance by their peers. A sense of belonging comes about in classrooms that are consistently well managed by qualified teachers. Classrooms that are free of put-downs and harassment lead to positive behaviors that are the prerequisites for success and growth. Students enter school with a wide range of predispositions toward education. However, a classroom climate that supports students through earned autonomy can mitigate negative predispositions (McNeely, Nonnemaker, & Blum, 2002)

Try to picture two classrooms, one where students are frequently buffeted by a hard–to-predict adult and one where risk taking is a prized attitude. Students in both classrooms ask many questions each day at an unconscious level:

- Is this teacher my friend or enemy?
- Will I be embarrassed or feel stupid?
- What will my classmates think?
- Can I do this work?
- Where is my connection to this task?
- Am I valued?

In the classroom where students cannot predict what they will get from a teacher, the answers to these questions may cause a student to disconnect from the adult and from learning. How can we expect learning if sarcasm, capricious decisions, and lack of respect are prevalent? In the classroom where it is comfortable to risk, there is a teacher who reinforces positive approximations, invites questions, is consistent and respectful, and allows students to earn autonomy through clearly stated and enforced guidelines. From such a base, a child can grow and learn. Belonging and connection can be measured in the level of risk a child is comfortable demonstrating.

Risk Taking

A toddler risks walking further and further away from a parent but frequently looks back to see if the parent is still present. The toddler has a clear limit to the toleration of distance from the parent. Each toddler's limit is unique and depends on a wide variety of factors. Similar factors continue to dominate our risk taking throughout life. Many of the factors are not static; they change over time, ebbing and flowing with life events. This most basic of psychological principles governs the potential to learn as well. Risk taking must be predicated by positive connections with others in the learning environment. Each time a child learns something new, the delicate balance of cognitive dissonance is tipped. When they develop a healthy level of risk taking, students encounter and work through cognitive dissonance despite problems. This cycle helps students build the necessary resiliency when things get hard or complicated, both in learning and in life (Burns, 1996).

The teacher who systematically establishes a climate that supports risk taking fills the environment with opportunities for connections with students. This also satisfies the needs of the social and emotional learning systems, which crave acceptance and inclusion in a safe environment. Practices that promote this type of environment contribute to teachers' abilities to form more meaningful relationships with students—relationships that pay off in students' increased motivation, learning, and academic achievement (McCombs & Whisler, 1997). In the rest of this chapter, we will give you key factors that help establish the essential conditions for learning in the educational environment of the classroom and allow you to differentiate for diverse learners.

ASSESSING THE LEARNING ENVIRONMENT

In books for beginning teachers, we frequently see excellent suggestions for establishing positive learning climates. We need to use these principles regularly, not just when we begin a teaching career or a school year. There are also numerous and inspiring books on factors needed to support the learning environment. Just as we check for understanding or assess writing, we need to develop ways to check that the classroom climate provides the connected atmosphere essential to learning.

Each student is unique, and we will need to differentiate how we provide these climatic factors, based on the data we collect. Creating a classroom climate that promotes learning is not a one-time proposition but rather a gentle series of adjustments every day. Great teachers make these adjustments unconsciously, yet conscious adjustments still are necessary to ensure that another 137 students will not be left behind.

There are several components that help us assess classroom climate. We have discussed the level of student risk taking. We also need to think about feedback, ritual, respect, cultural history, and celebration. So what are the key conditions that nurture, replicate, and sustain student growth? Learning is about the ability of the student to change and to grow, and so is teaching, by the way.

Without change, there can be no learning. The cognitive dissonance we pass through on the way to learning is the essence of change. Daryl Conner (1993) says the ability of people to change and learn has two key components. He notes that balancing the capability to change with the challenges we face is essential for change. When this balance is disturbed and capability exceeds challenge, we can become energized, although sustaining the energy over time is an issue. When challenge exceeds capability, individuals become overwhelmed, and that interferes with their resiliency. The highlighted conditions for a classroom climate that supports learning evolved from what we know about change and growth.

USING FEEDBACK

Mr. Norman comes into his classroom and notes that students seem uncertain about a current performance assessment they were working on in this unit. He notes that students are not as productive today. Students are wandering around the resource center. They are asking some pretty low-level compliance questions: for example, How many pages should I write? When is this assignment due? Since Mr. Norman is an excellent teacher, he observes student behaviors and takes mental temperature checks of climate at regular intervals.

Mr. Norman begins by asking students questions to further his understanding of the situation he observes. He asks some of the students if they know what to do next for the project. He also asks what is frustrating them. He asks them to talk through the work they started. Once he listens to students, Mr. Norman offers feedback on both their work and their thinking about the work. The atmosphere in the resource center changes as the energy level rises. Students seem to move and act with purpose, the questions change in quality, and students are again productive. Mr. Norman elevates "monitor and adjust" to a very impressive and useful level.

Effective Feedback

How does Mr. Norman know that feedback or the lack of it is the issue? Do all of the students respond to this adjustment, or do some still need more or different information? While part of feedback involves praise or correction, there is much more to it in a resilient classroom (Marzano et al., 2001). Ask yourself:

- What are the intuitive things the best teachers regularly watch for in the classroom to monitor their communication with students, especially the feedback level?
- What aspects of feedback build student resiliency for the continual changes needed to sustain learning?
- How do teachers know, from observing student behavior, that there is a problem specifically related to feedback?
- Which feedback remedies should be employed that reestablish student connections and the conditions for learning?

Students who feel in control and have a "can do" attitude demonstrate the ability to sustain change. A feedback process that is working (see Figure 1.1) helps students maintain a sense of control, reduces uncertainty, and encourages a higher level of thinking.

So what should a teacher look for if the amount, type, and content of the feedback in a classroom are working? Looking for these climate factors can help teachers evaluate

- Whether they need to change what they are doing
- What feedback they still need to provide
- Which students need additional feedback

These factors can assess other aspects of learning as well. Since proper feedback has such high payoff, starting with that aspect of classroom climate makes sense (Marzano et al., 2001).

Feedback That Promotes Reflective Thinking

Taking feedback in classrooms to the next level requires a teacher to ask students certain types of metacognition questions that could check many of these factors. Jim Bellanca describes his first awareness of metacognition from his fifth grade teacher, Mrs. Potter, who prompted students' reflections with the following questions after an assignment.

- What was I asked to do? What was my task?
- What did I do well? What was successful?
- If I were going to do this task again, what would I change or do differently?
- What help do I need?

These questions not only pushed students into their reflective learning system but facilitated goal setting, personal accountability, and advocacy.

Differentiating Feedback for Diverse Learners

What evidence confirms that feedback is not adequate? What are some of the things teachers can do to improve feedback? That depends on the type of students and their needs. Here are some examples from Rosabeth Kantor's (1985) work as well as the authors' 30-plus years of classroom observations and interactions.

Some of our starting points for feedback are common sense, others help teachers plan for careful and balanced approaches to feedback that increase student success and capacity. Feedback works when it makes connections real for students and honors the collaborative nature of a true student-centered classroom. Figure 1.2 can be copied and used to help you prompt the desired dialogue and interaction. The left-hand column

Figure 1.1 Observing If Feedback Is Working and Sufficient

- ❑ Students exhibit purposeful action

- ❑ Students can describe next steps

- ❑ Students can self-evaluate work in progress

- ❑ Students appropriately ask for assistance

- ❑ Students' questions are about aspects of complex thinking rather than procedure

- ❑ Students' attitude and demeanor are positive

- ❑ Students collaborate as needed without prompts

- ❑ Students positively reinforce each other through various types of interaction

- ❑ Students adhere to class norms

Figure 1.2 Customizing Your Feedback

Type of Student Needs and Behaviors	Starting Points for Teacher Feedback
Students who need to feel control	• Make certain feedback ends with a choice
Students who seem confused	• As you further explain the step the student is working on, clearly connect to the target • Use examples to make the parts-to-whole relationship evident • Try to ask questions about the personal impact of the issue or task
Students who seem anxious about specific learning tasks	• Reduce the surprise by referring back to the rubric or model • Break the steps of a task down into more achievable/quicker chunks
Students who seem embarrassed	• Eliminate any possible public conversation, keep it private • Allow students to choose from among a variety of acceptable methods to communicate learning
Students who cannot begin a project	• Structure and limit the choices and have students describe the one with the most advantages
Students who need frequent praise	• Teach them to self-evaluate using a checklist and have them bring you the list when multiple items have been checked off • Provide language for positive self-talk • Provide specific praise that celebrates a completed goal set by the student
Students who resist change in process or method	• Give them a connection to the previous process and a real-world rationale for the change • Have students suggest a viable method or process that does not compromise the standard or assessment
Students who seem angry about a task or issue related to the learning	• A private discussion around a "neutral source" (like evaluating a different student's work) may be necessary to reduce the intensity of the emotion • Have the student ask you questions; this lowers the threat level further
Students who seem bored	• This is an opportunity to refocus and let students start at a different point in the assignment or project or collaboratively reframe it until the meaning is more personal for them

describes student needs and behaviors, and the right-hand column suggests ways to use feedback to deal with each situation. This may be a handy chart to keep in your reflection book or journal as you consider specific students and their needs.

Feedback and praise that are planned and tuned to specific student behaviors and needs are far more effective than any generalized practice of generic praise and shotgun solutions. Specific praise allows a child to feel deeply connected, and that is a most powerful motivator (Kessler, 2000). Shotgun solutions are those generic reminders that a hurried teacher aims at a group. Customizing feedback to the moment and the student is far more effective. The collaboration of communication between a teacher and student is worth the time. It saves repetition, confused products, and disappointing results that in the long run cost more in terms of time, effort, and resources. Forging that personal connection and meeting student needs results in increased achievement and motivation.

RITUAL, RESPECT, AND CULTURAL HISTORY

Multiple teacher resources for beginning as well as veteran teachers talk about establishing norms for behavior and trying to enforce them consistently. Then what happens? What are the ongoing practices that continue to promote a healthy climate for learning?

Max Depree (1989) describes the use of ritual, and Terrence Deal and Kent Peterson (1998) have frequently explained the role of history in any social situation (institution) as essential preconditions for change and growth. So what do these elements look like in a classroom, and how does a teacher support a climate that encourages behaviors and attitudes for learning? See Boxes 1.1, 1.2, and 1.3 to get started.

Box 1.1 Ritual

Rituals provide a framework of predictability that is both comforting and foundational for risk taking. Rituals set forth a soothing path on which to build spiraling skills, even at the shaky beginning stages. Rituals can be about everyday rules of interaction and can also honor rites of passage and accomplishments; in this way, they establish a secure foundation for learning. Rituals cause a climate that won't rock or shake under the cognitive dissonance of effective learning.

Box 1.2 Respect

Respect requires an undisguised regard for both what makes us the same and what makes us different. Respect honors the human construction of a fabric that stretches out whenever a conversation or encounter takes place. All participants in an interaction or activity must hold up that fabric if honor and respect are to be continued. If one person drops the fabric, the conditions for success diminish as if we had turned off the engine of an automobile. Respect keeps a climate alive and moving forward, and for learning, moving forward is critical.

Box 1.3 Cultural History

Cultural histories establish the worth of each individual and group in the learning organization. While each individual brings to class a unique mix of the cultures that have affected his or her personality and behaviors, new cultures are formed with every encounter. The core of culture lies in stories we tell and the interpretation (visual or otherwise) of emotion colliding with events and circumstances. We create new stories and representations in a group that honors cultural history. Such histories also take into account the current community served by the school. Taking time in a classroom to describe the history of the group or the contributions of individuals and the group is a key component in establishing a growth-oriented classroom climate.

What does a classroom look like when all of these practices are in harmony and contributing to the climate for differentiation and growth of students? When assessing harmony and cohesiveness in human interaction, there are key characteristics that teachers can consider. Many popular and well-researched programs, for example, the Association for Supervision and Curriculum Development's *Character Education*, have some of these traits at the heart of their strategies. In this chapter, we focus on several traits that are common to these types of excellent programs, philosophies, and disciplines. These traits come from brain research, from safe and drug-free schools information, from discipline programs, from critical thinking research, and from several decades of experience with successful students and teachers. We could list a hundred traits. The ones we list in Figure 1.3 were chosen because they are consistent across many types of research literature and experiences of successful teachers and students. Each of these traits can be improved and sustained through

Figure 1.3 Seven Traits for Optimal Learning in a Positive Classroom Climate

Self-evaluation	The ability of a student to self-evaluate actions, products, and attitudes
Resiliency	The ability of a student to persevere regardless of failure
Adaptability	The ability of a student to respond with flexibility and to generalize learning across situations
Responsibility	The ability of a student to demonstrate accountability for actions, products, and attitudes
Teamwork	The ability of a student to function productively and positively as a member of a group
Competency	The ability of a student to feel a sense of worth resulting from academic and personal achievements
Expectation	The ability of a student to realistically judge the probability of positive and negative consequences and to take actions that influence a positive outcome

supportive and culturally sensitive rituals, demonstrations, and practice for ongoing and abiding respect and the honoring and communication of cultural history. The purpose of this particular list is to detail what teachers should look for as they assess the health and productivity level of their classroom. These traits, in our opinion, help create a classroom climate and culture conducive to learning. Figure 1.3 outlines the seven traits that help teachers assess climate so that a positive classroom environment can be maintained. A concise definition of each trait is also included.

We think these healthy climate characteristics describe the attributes of student behavior and thinking when ritual, respect, and cultural history have the impact we desire in classrooms. If teachers are going to create a healthy climate for learning, then these seven characteristics are needed to create the internal climate in individuals and the external climate or norms for groups. This condition creates a climate conducive to learning.

DIFFERENTIATING CLASSROOM CLIMATE

The teacher's role is to assess students with regard to these traits. Given information about these elements, teachers can then start to coach students and use ritual, respect, and cultural history to bring about desired change. These elements help teachers differentiate the affective as well as the academic expectations in a classroom. We find this type of model (see Figure 1.4) helpful in understanding the need to collect data and

Figure 1.4 Assessing Data About Student Traits for Optimal Learning in a Positive Classroom Climate

Student Traits for Optimal Learning	Evidence: What does the student do to demonstrate the trait?	Indicators for Data Collection: What would the student do or say in a positive classroom climate?	Differentiate Based on Analysis of the Data: What can be done if the student is not contributing to the class climate?
1. Self-evaluation	Uses criteria to self-evaluate	• Accurately describes personal behavior, action, or attitude • Generates a checklist for accomplishment, refining criteria with experience • Uses critical thinking and actions that help verify a process • Describes what will be different in the future • Is able to set a goal and work toward it • Uses clear or evolving criteria	*Ritual:* Describe what is seen rather than what is felt *Respect:* Establish a norm for taking care of personal needs and for regular self-reflection *Cultural History:* Use senses, learning styles, or multiple intelligences to clarify ideas or solutions
2. Resiliency	Demonstrates perseverance	• Is willing to try again • Learns from mistakes • Sticks with tasks and interactions • Refines a practice, given experience	*Ritual:* Write down a recent error and rip it up, placing pieces in an envelope along with a goal for next time; regularly check on goal progress *Respect:* Praise others who display perseverance *Cultural History:* Share stories from a variety of types of learners and cultures to help students see value and heroes who display this trait
3. Adaptability	Exhibits flexibility	• Can move to creative elaboration of ideas • Works through a constructivist task • Multitasks well	*Ritual:* Give feedback that values creative solution-oriented work habits and team behavior

(Continued)

Figure 1.4 (Continued)

Student Traits for Optimal Learning	Evidence: What does the student do to demonstrate the trait?	Indicators for Data Collection: What would the student do or say in a positive classroom climate?	Differentiate Based on Analysis of the Data: What can be done if the student is not contributing to the class climate?
		• Responds to different points of view positively • Can change his or her mind given new evidence, point of view, or purpose	Respect: Interview your group to establish strengths of each person Cultural History: Summarize the day's accomplishments through the story of each group or person
4. Responsibility	Maintains personal accountability	• Takes responsibility for actions • Works toward a goal • Adjusts work according to a model and/or rubric • Initiates tasks without multiple prompts • Exhibits internal personal control	Ritual: Revisit norms Respect: Write reflections and reframe questions and comments Cultural History: Pre-plan questions to ask a partner
5. Teamwork	Contributes to a group effort	• Actively seeks out the contributions of others • Sees the perspective of others by actively listening to other points of view • Is open to ideas and tolerant of the process • Takes turns • Supports the group effort and honors the needs of the group through collaboration	Ritual: Generate reasons for steps or group process Respect: Focus on solution generation Cultural History: Craft roles within group activities to clarify and hook personal contributions
6. Competency	Displays energy and motivation	• Describes what has to be accomplished • Communicates step-by-step arrival at a solution • Actively engages in activity or interaction • Asks good critical questions	Ritual: Reframe the goals of the interaction or function of the group Respect: Describe their role or contribution to reaching the goal

Student Traits for Optimal Learning	Evidence: What does the student do to demonstrate the trait?	Indicators for Data Collection: What would the student do or say in a positive classroom climate?	Differentiate Based on Analysis of the Data: What can be done if the student is not contributing to the class climate?
		• Encourages others • Learns from errors • Relates events to personal experience or application	*Cultural History:* Use peer assistance and evaluation
7. Expectation	Uses cause-and-effect analysis	• Elaborates reasons for a point of view • Asks complex questions of self and others • Identifies underlying causes • Sees consequences and possible interventions of solutions • Offers logical opinions and options	*Ritual:* End the day with a ticket out that explains the cause and effect of an action or new learning *Respect:* Reinforce student questions for growing insight and clarity *Cultural History:* Check assumptions through comparisons with past and current practice

differentiate our behavior to promote student learning. The student traits are listed in the left-hand column with a demonstrated example in the next column. Column three suggests student behaviors that can be used to assess the trait, and the last column suggests techniques to use to strengthen the trait.

These traits help teachers frame classroom climate. Using them frequently to assess the condition of classroom climate will allow teachers to make adjustments in the fabric of learning. Students with observant teachers, who make these minute course corrections on a frequent basis, will learn more and retain what they have learned to use it another day. The solutions and remedies listed using ritual, respect, and cultural history are just a sampling. Try your own. Share such solutions with other teachers and administrators. Such a list of tools and strategies will help you at any parent conference, student advocacy session, discipline intervention, or special needs conference, not to mention their impact on academic success.

Healthy classrooms increase the probability of student achievement. In classrooms where teachers model, reinforce, ask questions about, and spend time rehearsing these traits, the achievement level can be accelerated for learners from diverse backgrounds.

DIFFERENTIATING CELEBRATION AND PRAISE

There is nothing like a bit of fake and generalized praise to turn off a student and cause long-term distrust. We can watch teachers who use specific praise and see different results. Not all praise is created equal. Students must be able to believe the teacher and, more important, believe internally that the praise is earned and proportionate to the action or product eliciting the praise. A student who can self-reflect and self-evaluate will be able to connect with praise and use it more effectively as a confirmation of his or her own thinking (Kohn, 2002; Marzano et al., 2001). Praise should not be surprising to a student. So, how does a teacher help a student to attain a level of self-regard and evaluation that allows connection to celebrations of learning?

Before we can talk about celebration, we must talk about student thinking. Can students question their own assumptions, discover errors, and correct them, and can a student ask meaningful questions about the work? Listening to students and coaching these behaviors are essential to a student's ability to accept and believe praise. These same principles will be used again when we discuss student assessment in an upcoming chapter. These same areas help us assess student learning and differentiate teaching and learning based on the evidence we collect in these areas.

There are four primary areas in which we focus praise if we use a critical thinking model to facilitate growth and achievement in students (see Figure 1.5). These areas have been selected from a variety of research and work about critical thinking, higher order thinking skills, dimensions of learning, habits of the mind, Torrance's (1995) work on creativity, and psychology-based work on learning. While there are other areas of thinking that could help us focus and use celebration and praise well, the four elements outlined in Figure 1.5 are a good starting point. The left-hand column identifies the element to use for praise and celebration, and the right-hand column lists attributes in each category that should be praised in order to improve the rate of growth, performance, and learning.

Adjusting your praise to match thinking rather than task completion or expected compliance truly affects the climate for learning in a classroom. Does that mean you should not praise other things? Some students require a feedback approach from teachers that includes praise for task completion. However, save elaborate group celebrations of learning and public praise for higher-level thinking and watch student achievement rise.

Figure 1.5   Adjusting Praise and Celebrations in High-Achieving Classrooms

Focusing Elements for Praise and Celebration	What to Praise or Celebrate?
Fostering problem solving	Metacognition about problem solving and solution development Questioning the assumptions of self and others Discovering errors and understanding what aspects contribute to the error Discussing pros and cons of solutions
Extending elaboration Testing ideas and generalization	Finding evidence to support a point of view Developing criteria for evaluation Using prior learning to inform or form a new situation Using verbs in questions that indicate higher levels of thinking
Supporting creativity	Generating new ideas Shifting perspective easily and using data to adjust thinking Conceiving something new or using something in a unique way Building on other ideas Persevering even as difficulty levels rise
Developing schema	Describing the method of reaching an answer, solution, process, and so on Trying a strategy and acknowledging if it does not get the desired results, and then trying another strategy or seeking out a new method Using multiple strategies and solutions Using brainstorming, plus-minus-interesting, T-charts, pro and con, flow charting, mapping, creating a visual representation that is self-initiated rather than teacher initiated

SUMMARY

Classroom climate can be the key to learning. Without deep connections, predictable interactions, and self-reflection, student learning suffers. We can make observations, ask questions, and coach students in ways that increase the probability of learning and growth. Good teachers must assess climate and differentiate needed changes to accommodate various students. Test scores are only one factor in creating a body of evidence that allows us to make more meaningful and accurate choices about teaching and learning.

Each of the areas for focus and tools in this chapter is meant to heighten a teacher's awareness. It is difficult to differentiate if you do not pay attention to the climate of a classroom. Each teacher or school must make a decision about where to start. We will give you more ideas in this book that you can effectively use on particular occasions. Pick and choose your starting point. One teacher may start with monitoring feedback; another may like the idea of praise associated with higher level thinking skills. The key is in the observation and dialogue that takes place every day in every classroom. Classroom climate is a rich source of student data. We can use what we learn to adjust the achievement potential of each student.

Collecting Data to Know the Learner 2

It is important for learners to be aware of their strengths so that self-esteem and self-confidence are enhanced. It is important for teachers to have that knowledge, too, for planning, adjusting, and differentiating learning.

It is virtually impossible for teachers to plan for learning if they don't know the learner. Every student is unique, with a different background of experiences that have influenced brain circuitry and affected the connections that students make with new learning. Many theories exist that help us look at the uniqueness of the students we serve and the different intelligences that they possess. The key is to have strategies to gather the data we need about the uniqueness of each student and then to respond to that knowledge by creating a classroom and learning activities that will promote growth toward both targeted standards and student self-awareness.

It is imperative that we know the learner from a variety of angles. One view is examining learning styles and collecting student data about ways in which individual students learn and process information. Through learning styles and the data collected, we learn much about how the learner accesses, processes, and expresses information and skills.

GOING WITH THE FLOW

Knowing how and when students are in "flow" is a way of tapping into their personalities to hook them into the learning. Flow is the term coined by Mihaly Csikszentmihalyi (1990) for the condition that exists when challenge and feedback are matched and learners are engaged in meaningful relevant activities without concern for time or reward. We might liken this to being "in the groove."

Think about a teacher who walks around the classroom and notices that students are not productive or have numerous procedural questions. A good teacher will recognize that the flow of learning is not evident. That teacher may reiterate directions, give additional examples, or continue individual coaching of students until the flow of learning is reestablished.

Teaching is sometimes like riding a bobsled; we need to stay in a certain groove on the icy course to maximize the speed and smoothness of a run. Minor course corrections can mean the difference between winning and losing. In teaching, knowing when to make those corrections is essential and often a topic among new teachers. However, understanding what kind of course correction will get a student or group of students back into that running groove of learning is harder to accomplish.

Each member of the bobsled team has a specific set of strengths that are relied on for smooth running. Helping students understand both strengths and style differences allows them to participate with the teacher in needed course changes. In this chapter, we will focus on collecting data that helps us know the learner well enough to recognize the need for course corrections, and we will present some ideas about what kind of corrections may establish the best groove for learning. We will also discuss how learners can get to know needs that will help them self-select learning approaches.

DIFFERENT LEARNING STYLES

Our first step is to understand and recognize different types of learning styles. Four theorists have independently developed a learning styles profile system. Each system has characteristics that fall into four major categories, as shown in Figure 2.1, although each theorist calls the category by a different name. However, when the four categories are compared, they contain similar attributes. The names of their categories can be difficult to recall and often don't give the complete picture and understanding of the style.

In *Differentiated Instructional Strategies: One Size Doesn't Fit All*, Gregory and Chapman (2002) used the analogies of Clipboards, Microscopes, Puppies, and Beach Balls to identify the four learning styles. The objects were selected to help us visualize and to more clearly suggest how different learners process information, as outlined in Figure 2.1. Each of these objects has certain attributes that also describe the type of learner that it represents. Using these analogies, we can create a single mental file that holds all the attributes of the style and is more easily remembered (see Figure 2.2).

Consider using a self-reflection inventory as shown in Figure 2.3 as a way to help students identify their learning styles and to help teachers collect data for use in planning. Ask the students to read each statement in

Figure 2.1 A Matrix of Learning Styles Illustrates Their Connections and Similarities

	Gregorc, 1982	Kolb, 1984	Silver et al., 2000	4Mat/McCarthy
Beach Ball	Concrete Random • Divergent • Experiential • Inventive	Accommodator • Likes to try new ideas • Values creativity, flexibility, and risk takers	Self-Expressive • Feelings to construct new ideas • Produces original and unique materials	Type 4 Dynamic • Create and act • Usefulness and application of learning
Clipboard	Concrete Sequential • Task oriented • Efficient • Detailed	Converger • Values what is useful and relevant, immediacy, and organizing essential information	Mastery • Absorbs information concretely, and processes step by step	Type 3 Common Sense • Think and do • Active, practical • Make things work
Microscope	Abstract Sequential • Intellectual • Analytical • Theoretical	Assimilator • Avid readers who seek to learn • Patience for research • Values concepts	Understanding • Prefers to explore ideas and use reason and logic based on evidence	Type 2 Analytical • Reflect and think • Observers who appreciate lecture methods
Puppy	Abstract Random • Imaginative • Emotional • Holistic	Diverger • Values positive, caring environments that are attractive, comfortable, and people-oriented	Interpersonal • Appreciates concrete ideas and social interaction to process and use knowledge	Type 1 Imaginative • Feel and reflect • Create and reflect on an experience

the inventory and to color in the boxes that best describe them. The first set of statements shows preferences related to beach balls, the second to puppies, the third to clipboards, and the fourth to microscopes.

Figures 2.4 through 2.7 allow us to examine each style for its related strengths, needs, attitudes, and preferences. It's not that we want to label students or identify their learning styles and then cater to those styles. It's

Figure 2.2 Preferences of Different Learning Styles

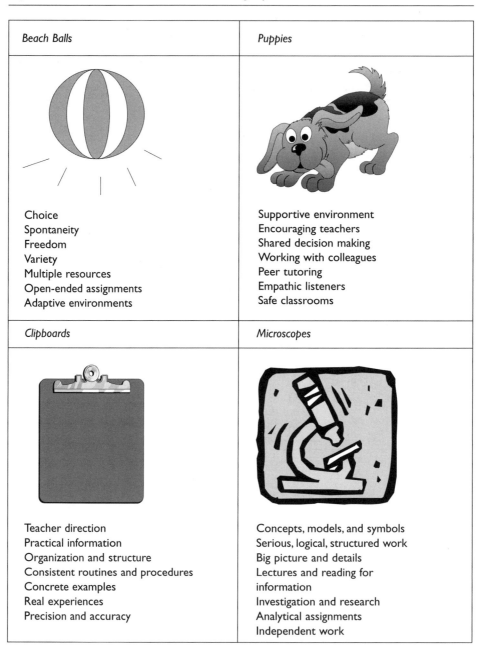

Beach Balls	Puppies
Choice Spontaneity Freedom Variety Multiple resources Open-ended assignments Adaptive environments	Supportive environment Encouraging teachers Shared decision making Working with colleagues Peer tutoring Empathic listeners Safe classrooms
Clipboards	Microscopes
Teacher direction Practical information Organization and structure Consistent routines and procedures Concrete examples Real experiences Precision and accuracy	Concepts, models, and symbols Serious, logical, structured work Big picture and details Lectures and reading for information Investigation and research Analytical assignments Independent work

that we want to be aware of what all learners need and consider how we can build in those needs in the classroom. We also want students to recognize their own styles so that they are conscious of their strengths and can advocate for what they need to be successful and engaged in

Figure 2.3 Self-Reflection Inventory

Read each statement and color in the boxes that are most like you.

❏ I like new challenges
❏ I like creating and discovering
❏ I like new things and ideas
❏ I like to use my imagination
❏ I like moving about
❏ I like music and art
❏ I like to think about where new information can lead me
❏ Total _____

❏ I like to work with my friends
❏ I like group work in class
❏ I like everyone to feel good
❏ I like helping other people
❏ I like everyone to succeed
❏ I try to understand how others feel
❏ I like to share ideas and problems
❏ Total _____

❏ I like to follow directions
❏ I like routines each day
❏ I like to finish a job or assignment
❏ I like to see models and make things
❏ I like to do things I feel comfortable with
❏ I like to follow patterns
❏ I like to solve problems step by step
❏ Total _____

❏ I like to examine things that interest me
❏ I like to understand how things work
❏ I like to think and solve problems
❏ I like to read to get the information I need
❏ I like to organize things so they make sense to me
❏ I like to see the details and parts
❏ I like to play with ideas, new models, and projects
❏ Total _____

Figure 2.4 Learning Style of Beach Balls

Strengths	Needs
Experimentation Risk taking Adventurous Intuitive and insightful Creative Spontaneous	Guidelines Boundaries Expectations Standards Parameters Help in focusing
Attitudes	*Preferences*
Don't like step-by-step directions React to internal and external rewards Want to improve things for society	Stimulus-rich environment Options and alternatives Interesting and exciting learning

Figure 2.5 Learning Style of Puppies

Strengths	Needs
Empathic Intuitive Subjective, abstract, affective Read between the lines See the gestalt	Opportunities to work with others Time for self-reflection To connect with teacher and other learners Rationale for learning
Attitudes	*Preferences*
Internal motivation Self-monitoring toward personal criteria Require rationale for learning Can block out stimuli	Subjective versus abstract Personal incentives, encouragement Choice of learning environments

the learning. Knowing themselves also helps them to understand that when they are frustrated or anxious, it may be related to their style. This will allow and facilitate the reflective theater to be activated for metacognition.

Figure 2.6 Learning Style of Microscopes

Strengths	Needs
See the big picture Home in on main points Learn from lecture and reading Think in abstract terms and language Analyze theories and information Thorough logical learners Can delay gratification	Help in working with others Help in organizing time and bringing closure
Attitudes	*Preferences*
Don't like to waste time "pooling ignorance" Don't like inquiry	Vicarious learning Simulations Analytical thinking Expert information Feedback that will improve grades

Student Self-Reflection and Journaling About Their Learning Styles

Asking students to use a journal to reflect on a task or learning experience can help them be more conscious and in control of their learning. Some journal prompts may include the following:

- Today I worked on . . .
- It was difficult to . . .
- I really enjoyed . . .
- If I could make one wish . . .
- If I could change one thing . . .
- Next time I would . . .
- It would help me if . . .

Figure 2.7 Learning Style of Clipboards

Strengths	Needs
Precision and accuracy Striving for perfection Practicality Compliance with teacher Sensory responsive Externally motivated Delay gratification	Real experiences Concrete examples, not theories Structure Procedures, routines Directions
Attitudes	Preferences
No news is good news Serious about their work Require feedback	Precise, useful feedback Recommendations Appreciate privacy

Figure 2.8 is a chart that may serve as a guide for students to reflect on and project their learning needs.

Teaching for Different Learning Styles

We ultimately want students to be able to advocate for their own learning and be mindful of what they need to continue to grow. But it is also important for teachers to satisfy the learning needs for each learning style.

Beach Balls. Teachers can satisfy the learning needs of beach balls by offering choices and options for experimentation and creativity. But they also must recognize that these learners need deadlines, guidelines, and boundaries or else they may have trouble focusing or completing assignments. These skills are useful not just in school but also in life.

Clipboards. It's also important for clipboards to have order, structure, and routine with clear guidelines and expectations. What will happen when the unexpected occurs? They also need to break out of the routine and learn to deal with ambiguity, spontaneity, and anomalies. Life isn't always routine or predictable. Dealing with the unexpected is also a life skill.

Figure 2.8 Self-Reflection Journal

Reflecting on . . .	I realize . . .	Request . . .

Microscopes. Microscopes like to analyze and investigate the truth they seek. Will they have time to go as deeply as they need for their learning? They also need help in working with others, developing collaborative skills, and seeing other people's point of view.

Puppies. Puppies are great collaborative learners and enjoy partner and group work, but they also need to develop independent skills and to take risks and venture forth in new areas on their own.

We can include all learners if we do the following:

1. *Substantiate or rationalize the learning as a desirable skill or knowledge needed.* Why? Give them a reason for learning. Connect to their world.

2. *Give them the facts. Provide models and concepts. Time to explore.* What? The substance and content are clearly exposed, shared, and examined.

3. *Provide time for application.* Let students practice with the skill or knowledge and find practical uses for it. How does this work? Experimentation and application in practical ways.

4. *Offer outlets for creativity for dynamic interaction with the material and skills.* So what? Students select opportunities to transfer the new learning to new situations.

DIFFERENT INTELLIGENCES

Gardner's Multiple Intelligences

Another way of looking at how we are smart is to examine Howard Gardner's (1993) multiple intelligences. By adding an *s* to intelligence, Gardner broadened how we look at it. According to Gardner, intelligent people

- Solve problems
- Handle crises
- Create things of value in a particular culture

using a variety of ways of accessing, processing, and applying information.

Sternberg's Triarchic Model

Gardner's theory meshes well with Robert Sternberg's (1996) triarchic model. Sternberg suggests that successful intelligence is the ability to use knowledge with creative intelligence, analytic intelligence, and practical intelligence. Knowledge in and of itself is nice, but to be truly valuable, it must be used in an intelligent way.

Creative intelligence. We use the cognitive processes to create questions, problems, and projects that validate new learning. This frequently involves challenging existing assumptions and removing obstacles in our quest for new ways to do things. It is really like "thinking outside the box."

Analytic intelligence. This type of thinking is used to analyze new learning and use it to solve problems, make choices, and judge critically. It includes the ability to identify a problem, create strategies, offer solutions, muster resources, monitor their application, and evaluate results. Educational testing often focuses on this form of intelligence.

Practical intelligence. This is the pragmatic intelligence that jumps into action with new information to use it in a practical way. Action oriented, this intelligence helps us to get on with things by putting the learning to good use to solve problems and make decisions. This may be referred to as "street smarts" and real-world application.

Thus in classrooms, we can challenge students not only to learn information but also to use that information in a practical, analytical, and creative way. For example, if students are studying the topic of nutrition, they may take their new knowledge and apply it in a *practical* way by creating a healthy diet for themselves or someone with a particular dietary need. They may *analyze* their own meals for a week to assess their nutritional health. *Creatively,* they could design a restaurant menu based on their knowledge that would be nutritionally sound as well as delicious and appealing. Figure 2.9 shows how that unit might be approached using the triarchic model.

Figure 2.9 Applying New Knowledge: Sample Unit on Nutrition

Unit or Topic: Nutrition

Content: Food Sources of Nutrients

Creative	Analytical	Practical
Students could *design* a healthy restaurant menu based on their knowledge that would be nutritionally sound as well as delicious and appealing.	They may *analyze* their own meals for a week to assess their nutritional health.	They may apply knowledge in a *practical* way by creating a healthy diet for themselves or someone with a particular dietary need.

This approach also will engage different types of learners because of their learning styles or multiple intelligences. As you think about your next unit of study, use Figure 2.10 to consider how you might build in a practical, analytical, and creative approach to processing new information.

Figure 2.10 Applying New Knowledge

Unit or Topic: _____

Content: _____

Creative	Analytical	Practical

Howard Gardner proposes that people are intelligent if the can solve problems, handle crises, and produce things of value in their culture. According to Gardner (1993), the first two intelligences are the *communication* intelligences:

- Verbal/linguistic
- Musical/rhythmic

The next four are referred to as *object-related* intelligences:

- Logical/mathematical
- Visual/spatial
- Bodily/kinesthetic
- Naturalist

The last two deal with *the self*:

- Interpersonal
- Intrapersonal

Teaching for Different Intelligences

We all posses these intelligences in varying degrees. Teachers sometimes take an in-depth look at each intelligence individually.

They may help students understand each intelligence and create a slogan for it, then stimulate that intelligence through a variety of activities and have students reflect on the experiences.

Teachers might take a new intelligence each week and focus on its strengths, preferences, and pitfalls, then identify famous people who have these intelligences and careers that draw on these strengths. Bulletin boards (see Figure 2.11), for example, can be used to focus on the intelligence for the week, profiling people and skills reflected by people with this intelligence. Figure 2.12 offers a definition for each type of intelligence, a slogan that might describe it, and some ways to cultivate it in the classroom. Teachers can also build in application of the multiple intelligences in any content area in a variety of ways, as shown in Figure 2.13.

Gardner's (1993) bodily/kinesthetic intelligence aligns closely with the physical learning system. Allowing and facilitating students to tap into their physical theater opens another avenue for their thinking and processing of information. Hands-on learning and kinesthetic activities deepen students' understanding of new learning in a concrete way.

To help students reflect on these eight intelligences, teachers can take time to examine learning activities each day and have students plot them

Figure 2.11 Sample Bulletin Board for the Week

Intelligence: _____

Strengths: Things Done Well or Easily	Challenges: Things That Don't Come Easily
Famous People With This Intelligence	Careers With This Intelligence

on a graph (Figure 2.14). This also taps into the reflective learning system and allows students to consider their learning, set goals, and review their learning and the processes that work for them.

This type of student reflection is also an excellent source of informal data for a teacher to use when adjusting learning and teaching strategies to meet specific needs. After each learning experience, take the time to plot the activity in one cube of the column that reflects the intelligence that was used. Then students can comment on how they enjoyed the activity or were frustrated or discouraged by it.

This also helps teachers to see visually which intelligences have garnered the most attention that week. For example, if students have just finished a mind map on the battles of the Civil War, they might include that in one cube of the visual/spatial column and also in one cube of the logical/mathematical column. Students could then write a reflection about it using the journal format (Figure 2.8), or they could write about whether the activity was Positive, Minus, or Interesting (De Bono, 1987), as shown in Figure 2.15.

Students might also use a class circle and a wraparound reflection. They could sit in a circle and each might respond with

- Two words that would describe the experience
- What kind of intelligence they used and how they felt about it

Figure 2.12 Examining Multiple Intelligences

Definitions	Slogans	Cultivation of Intelligences
Verbal/linguistic. Using language to read, write, and speak to communicate	Just say it!	• Play word games for vocabulary • Practice explaining ideas • Tell jokes and riddles • Play trivial pursuit • Make up limericks
Musical/rhythmic. Communicate in rhyme and rhythm	Get with the beat!	• Interview people about their favorite music • Make up a song about your favorite things • Play "name that tune" • Create a class song • Share poems that are special to you
Logical/mathematical. Use logic and reason to solve problems	Plot your course!	• Introduce graphic organizers to students and let them reflect on their use • Offer logic problems or situations and have students share problem-solving strategies
Visual/spatial. Ability to visualize in our mind's eye	Picture in your mind!	• Offer students opportunities to close their eyes and visualize: scenes, processes, and events • Allow and encourage students to add drawings and representations in their work or demonstrate understanding
Bodily/kinesthetic. Ability to learn and to express oneself through the whole body	I do, I understand!	• Let students role-play processes and events • Create a dance or mime to illustrate a new learning • Create gestures or actions that demonstrate new learning
Naturalist. Ability to recognize and classify	Mother Nature knows!	• Provide students with opportunities to classify and examine learning for like or different attributes • Allow students time for examination and a closer look
Intrapersonal. Ability to be self-reflective	Looking back, looking ahead!	• Ask students to think about a plan for their assignment or to reflect on the process and set goals for improvement • Introduce journals or reflection time so students reflect on their work and their thinking

Definitions	Slogans	Cultivation of Intelligences
Interpersonal. Ability to work with others	Together is better!	• Practice positive skills of active listening, encouragement • Show appreciation for the "smarts" of others

Figure 2.13 Applying Multiple Intelligences

Gardner's Intelligences Described	Applications in Any Content Area
Verbal/linguistic. Developing communication skills that include reading, writing, listening, speaking, and connecting information	Write Report Explain Describe and discuss Interview Label Give and follow directions
Musical/rhythmic. Communication and sensitivity to rhythm, rhyme, and music	Chant Sing Enjoy raps and songs Beat a rhythm Poetry Limericks Ballads
Logical/mathematical. Organizing information through logical abstract thinking focusing on numbers and patterns	Advance organizers Graphic organizers Puzzles Debates Critical thinking Graphs and charts Data and statistics
Visual/spatial. Working with visualization and spatial relationships involving color, space, and media	Draw Create Visualize Paint Imagine Make models Describe in detail

(Continued)

Figure 2.13 (Continued)

Gardner's Intelligences Described	Applications in Any Content Area
Bodily/kinesthetic. Using the mind/body connections through use of movement, tactile and kinesthetic processes	Perform Create Construct Develop Manipulate Dance or mime
Naturalist. Being attuned to nature and recognizing the patterns and classification therein	Classify, sort Organize using criteria Investigate Analyze Identify, categorize
Intrapersonal. Independent work through self-direction, goal setting, and metacognition	Metacognition Logs and journals Independent study Goal setting Positive affirmations Autobiography Personal questions
Interpersonal. Cooperative work incorporating empathic social interaction	Groupwork Partner activities Reciprocal teaching Peer reading, editing, counseling Role play Class meetings Conferencing and sharing

- A song that would be appropriate for the lesson
- How the lesson was important or how they will use the information

The teacher might reflect on the following:

- How did this learning experience engage learners?
- Were the objectives met?
- Which students were not engaged?
- What would I change for the next time?
- What could I add to reach more learners and increase success?

Figure 2.14 Weekly Observation of Students' Multiple Intelligences Activities

Student Profile	
Observing Over Time . . .	*Name:* _____
Verbal/Linguistic	Intrapersonal
Logical/Mathematical	Visual/Spatial
Interpersonal	Bodily/Kinesthetic
Musical/Rhythmic	Naturalist

SOURCE: Reprinted from *Differentiated Instruction Strategies: One Size Doesn't Fit All,* by Gayle H. Gregory and Carolyn Chapman.

STUDENT CONTRACTING FOR REFLECTIVE LEARNING

It is important that students learn to self-advocate. One way to practice and let students begin to adjust for their own style of learning is to use various forms of contracting, like the sample contract shown in Figure 2.16.

Figure 2.15 Student Reflection About Learning Experiences

Positive	Minus	Interesting

SOURCE: Adapted from De Bono, 1987.

Older students may choose to write their own contracts along lines similar to the one shown in Figure 2.16. Contracting is an important component to help some students begin rehearsing self-evaluation. It is often easier for them to start with their individual learning style needs than with their schoolwork. Other forms of contracting may help students to adjust concepts, skills, or questions and other factors during the unit. While many teachers formulate contracts for behavior or for student learning, it is also effective to have students design their own contracts if self-evaluation is the goal.

INTELLIGENT BEHAVIORS

Many theorists postulate what they think intelligence is. Art Costa (Costa & Garmston, 1994), for example, proposes that being intelligent is knowing what to do when you don't know what to do. Dr. Costa proposes twelve intelligent behaviors that help us with our thinking:

- *Persistence.* To persist in spite of obstacles or frustrations to find solutions to dilemmas or problems
- *Decreasing Impulsivity.* To control physical and emotional responses in order to be successful in a situation
- *Empathic listening.* To feel for another by putting oneself "in their shoes," evoking the thoughts and feelings that they might be experiencing
- *Metacognition.* To be aware of one's own thinking and to revisit or reflect on situations, challenges, or problems
- *Flexibility in thinking.* To be able to adjust to, try out, and explore other points of view

Figure 2.16 Sample Student Learning Contract

Learning Contract

I need help! My name is: _____

I have marked the kinds of help I need.

How I need to show what I have learned:	What types of time and work would help me finish my assignment:
Headphones	Extra Time
Record Work	Fewer Items
Use a Computer	
Work With a Partner	New Work

What kind of resources and materials do I need:	What else would help me be successful: *(Write or draw what you need!)*
Extra Help From My Teacher	
Use the Internet	
Different Materials	

This is OK with me.

Teacher _____ Date _____

- *Checking for accuracy and precision.* To know what quality looks like and to monitor one's progress toward quality, including correctness and clarity
- *Posing of questions and problems.* To continue to inquire and uncover new information that extends one's learning
- *Drawing on past experience to new situations.* To reflect on past experiences, recognizing the value of transfer to a different scenario
- *Using precise and accurate language.* To use specific descriptive language that conveys correct definitions for ideas and concepts
- *Using all senses.* To explore one's environment using all the senses in order to fully understand new things and information
- *Creativity.* To take one's knowledge and skills and explore solutions to problems in ways that have not been tried before
- *Sense of efficacy as a thinker.* To move from timidity to confidence and passion about thinking and learning

Some teachers feature these twelve behaviors on a bulletin board and refer to a particular behavior as students are working on an assignment or project. Identifying what the behavior looks like, sounds like, and feels like may be useful to help students understand the behavior and to give them language that supports it. For example, if persistence were the intelligent behavior being discussed, creating a visual organizer like the one shown in Figure 2.17 might be helpful. Each behavior, if mastered, will serve the individual well by enriching opportunities for thinking, problem solving, and human interaction. The behaviors might also be more evident in one style than another. Our goal would be to identify these behaviors and help students develop all of them to the best of their ability (see Figure 2.18).

REFLECTIONS

Here are reflections by a group of teachers in Idaho who saw things this way:

> Learning by doing is what we need.
> Hearing words only plants the seed.
> Sitting at our desks can really be a bore.
> Writing all day is a terrible chore.
> Give us a game, give a play.
> The learning sinks in much better that way.
> Get us out of our seats, keep us on the move.
> Helps us learn easily, keeps us in the groove.

Create your own reflective tool or use the one we created as Figure 2.19 to reflect on how you can do your best to know every learner in your classroom.

Figure 2.17   Sample Visual Organizer for Intelligent Behaviors

Behavior: Persistence

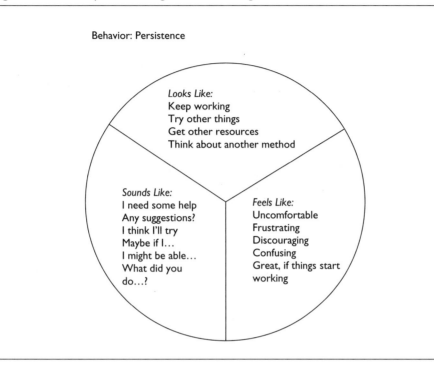

Looks Like:
Keep working
Try other things
Get other resources
Think about another method

Sounds Like:
I need some help
Any suggestions?
I think I'll try
Maybe if I...
I might be able...
What did you
do...?

Feels Like:
Uncomfortable
Frustrating
Discouraging
Confusing
Great, if things start
working

SOURCE: Adapted from Hill and Hancock, 1993.

Figure 2.18   Intelligent Behaviors and Learning Styles

Beach Balls	*Puppies*
Flexibility in thinking Posing questions and problems Drawing on past experiences Creativity	Empathic listening Using all senses
Clipboards	*Microscopes*
Checking for accuracy and precision Precise and accurate language Using all the senses Decreasing impulsivity	Persistence Metacognition Sense of efficacy as a thinker

Figure 2.19 Reflections on Becoming: Looking Back, Looking Ahead

- What is it that you are already doing to get to know the learner?

- What ideas in particular intrigued you and might you want to investigate further?

- What strategies from this chapter would be helpful in gathering data about the uniqueness of your students?

- What type of record keeping will you or your students use to collect and reflect on the data?

- What metacognitive opportunities can you offer your students and yourself as you collect data about the learners?

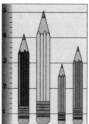

Collecting and Using Assessment Data for Diagnostic Teaching

3

An assessor is one who listens and advises, according to the dictionary. *Assessment* is a very old word. Assessors sat with an individual being taxed while visiting the home or business to determine and advise on the value and worth of possessions *and* their potential. In education today, the word *assessment* has come to mean a test score on an instrument determined by the state or final and summative assessments. While the current interpretation may be a fact of life when student growth and not taxation is the issue, we need to revisit the older origins of this word. An assessor listened to a business owner and wrote down a current valuation for the property and possessions. In addition, the assessor made notes, often in the margins of a small ledger, about the potential for this business and at what point to visit again.

Let us translate this image of an assessor to the educational environment. What if we listened to our students and observed what they now possess in the way of skills? Could we set a goal or a valuable growth target for this student? Could that help us determine a starting point for learning and help us differentiate the learning to reach the necessary growth for this student? Then, we could make a note to come back to this role of listening and observing at regular intervals to determine if the growth is actually occurring. By checking for growth at certain intervals, we would increase the likelihood that our assessment and the learning environment are producing the desired results for students. If not, minor corrections could be made along the way. By placing the teacher in the role of assessor, we make far more progress than by using a single test score as our sole measure of value.

DIAGNOSTIC TEACHING

The diagnostic thinking of teachers, every day in every classroom, is most likely to increase the probability that students will grow and achieve. Checking at intervals and making adjustments in student learning and teaching will have high payoffs for student achievement. However, it is one thing to note progress or the lack of progress and another thing to know what to do next. True diagnostic thinking requires teachers to reflect consciously on student learning and then connect their conclusions to the most effective next steps. In this chapter, we hope to describe clearly those regular assessments of learning and their connections to effective strategies.

The best teachers make minor course corrections every day in their classrooms. By taking the right approach to assessment, they can take the next steps toward the results and growth they want for their students. This will take good listening and observation skills and a clear knowledge of the desired result. In our classrooms, assessors should be top-notch observers of student potential; they should be able to turn the direction of teaching and learning on a dime to maximize growth. This is possible to do whether you have 24 kindergartners or 150 U.S. history students a day or 65 students in your physical education classroom each period. With the right tools and logical connections to strategies, teachers can increase the accuracy of instruction and student learning and thereby increase academic growth.

PRE-ASSESSMENT

In the pre-standards era of assessment, Form A of the final test was often used as a pre-assessment prior to instruction. Form B was the final assessment after instruction. This was thought to be the only way to assess growth. However, in a world of standards-based performance assessments, Form A and B no longer make sense. A performance assessment may take the entire unit to complete, or it may take several days at the end of a unit. It is not possible to replicate the summative assessment in this case. So, what are the other ways to pre-assess, and how do we analyze this type of data to make effective decisions about the next steps in student learning?

Some of the original research on pre-assessment was done with prisoners and with preschoolers. This 1950s and 1960s research focused on nationally standardized measures and used the Form A and Form B approach

(Rickard & Stiles, 1985). The information in this research measured the summative growth on standardized information or skills but did little that informed daily instruction. Later research, especially with preschoolers and special education students, did give teachers a profile to work from and a list of skills to teach; however, teachers were not given information about how to teach or how students would best learn (Cunningham, 1999).

The biggest changes in thinking about pre-assessment came about with the upswing in research about the brain, learning styles, multiple intelligences, mathematics, and literacy. A recent study in math published in Britain (Williams & Ryan, 2000) truly characterizes the latest shift away from the traditional pre-assessment and toward diagnostic thinking. Diagnostic thinking is the ability of a teacher to gather key information about learners and then make instructional decisions. Those decisions involve what and how to teach and how students should learn to demonstrate the subsequent steps or skills. A diagnostic teacher truly exemplifies our model of a modern assessor, using a variety of methods to determine current skill level and potential in order to make more accurate decisions about student learning. The greater the accuracy of the selection of instruction and student learning strategies, the greater the potential is for a student to reach proficient or higher levels of performance (Orlich et al., 1980).

There are teachers who still think

- Pre-assessment is a waste of time.
- Some students won't know it, so they might as well teach it anyway.
- They don't have time to adjust the learning because there is so much to cover.
- They don't know what to do with the data from the pre-assessment.
- They are very happy with the way they teach the material now.

Instead of that pattern, let us look at three math classrooms (Boxes 3.1, 3.2, and 3.3) to better understand the potential of a diagnostic teacher.

Box 3.1 Classroom 1

In the first math classroom, students are not given a pre-assessment of any kind. The teacher feels that the students "need" the next chapter of the text. This teacher "feels" that most students will know only a few things about the current topic, say fractions. Giving any assessment prior to the next chapter will be a waste of time. In this class, some students will reach proficient performance, while many others will not. This teacher may feel that it is solely up to the students to benefit from what and how the material is taught.

Box 3.2 Classroom 2

In the second classroom, the teacher wants to pre-assess and therefore uses an algorithm-based assessment before and after the unit. This teacher is pleased that all students did better after the unit or chapter than before.

Box 3.3 Classroom 3

In the third classroom, the teacher gets groups of two and three students working on a problem that uses some of the skills and concepts from the previous unit and introduces a concept or two from the next unit. The teacher gives students time to think and work together to develop creative ways to approach the problem. The teacher walks around the room and takes some notes.

We would predict that each teacher will get a different result. Studies show that the third teacher will plan instruction more accurately than the others and therefore increase the likelihood that more students will demonstrate proficient or better performance on the final assessment. The British research in math (Williams & Ryan, 2000) tells us that regardless of grade level, one of the best ways to plan in mathematics is to listen to students' adaptive reasoning and use of numeracy concepts as they apply them in realistic ways.

Teachers can listen for flawed reasoning, incomplete concept formation, or incorrect assumptions. From this information, teachers can plan how many students might benefit from manipulatives, computer-assisted training, advanced organizers, different types of grouping, and other methods as the unit progresses through the introductory phase. Teachers may also discover whether the misinformation students have is interfering with application and understanding. This is only one way of effectively diagnosing student learning prior to instruction. Each student will still be required to demonstrate adequate performance on the final standards-based assessment.

Diagnostic thinking gives teachers information that will help them think about timing, materials, depth of thinking, and methods in the upcoming unit. Such thinking does not necessarily require a teacher to individualize instruction, but it does help a teacher to offer a variety of methods and approaches over time for all students.

Figure 3.1   Content Areas and Pre-assessment Methods

Content Area	Primary Focus Areas of Concepts and Skills for Pre-Assessment	Ways to Pre-Assess or Diagnose Current Student Knowledge and Skills
English, history, reading, foreign language, and other humanities	Note skills in communication, attainment of concepts, and levels of critical thinking	Journal entry, dialogue, previous written product, short essay, word completion, oral response, anecdotal records, communication checklist
Math and science	Note a process, application of processes, understanding of a constant or theory	Process explanation or utilization, observation of a process, solving a problem, demonstration, short essay, sequencing steps, citing solution method with a rationale or process checklist
Music, art, physical education, and other performance based subjects	Observe a technique and complex application of skills	Performance observation, demonstration, participation level, techniques checklist
Computer science, industrial technology, business applications, and other career courses	Observe the complex integration of skills to solve a problem or develop a product	Performance observation, demonstration, skills checklist for a product or problem solution, sequencing steps

SOURCE: Adapted from Kuzmich, 1998.

Designing Diagnostic Opportunities

Designing a diagnostic opportunity will look very different in some ways depending on what content area you are assessing. We need to create diagnostic opportunities that match what we are trying to accomplish in each area (Roeber, 1996). Figure 3.1 can help us discuss what these big ideas are and how we use them in each content area.

Designing Diagnostic Assessments

How do we assess the gap between what we know about students and what performance is expected of them for the final assessment of the next unit? And how should a teacher decide on a method for pre-assessment? There are three questions that help us get there.

1. What do I know about my students now?

2. What is the nature and content of the final assessment for this unit or period of time?

3. What don't I know about the content knowledge, the critical thinking, and the process or skill demonstration of my students?

Using those questions, we can design a type of simple pre-assessment that will help us know what lies in the gap between where students are now and what they will need to do for the final assessment. Let us look at an example.

After the first couple of days of a unit, a grade school teacher or a secondary language arts teacher may already have some idea of how well a student writes a short and longer constructed response. This may be a few words in first grade or a series of sentences. It could be multiple paragraphs in middle school and fully elaborated essays in high school. Advanced students may not follow an expected developmental level. So, let us try out an example. Given a unit on persuasive writing, where students will research and write a persuasive report or essay on the final assessment:

1. What does the gap in what the teacher may know about the students look like?

2. What will the teacher do with the information that is gathered?

So what does the gap look like between what we know and where we want students to go?

- We may not know the students' clarity in thinking about the topic for research or concepts associated with persuasive writing.
- We may not know if they have the depth of thinking to create persuasive writing.
- We do have information about how they write.

So we could create a pre-assessment that involves a short persuasive paragraph, or we could use an advanced organizer that helps us learn about students' reasoning. The information from this pre-assessment could help us determine

1. How much time we need to spend describing the concepts of persuasive writing and the research topic or coaching students on the use of these writing concepts and developing their thinking skills through various types of questioning

2. How to adjust the topic choice

3. How much rehearsal to provide regarding claims or position statements, and so on

4. Which students are more or less independent in learning about writing

This type of pre-assessment

- Does not necessarily have to be graded
- Is not always designed for feedback
- Is designed to inform planning

Such writing could be sorted into three or four groups depending on the result, or teachers could make notes as students complete this short task. This type of information helps us provide differentiation opportunities for students. If we use the information for student feedback, students could develop goals for what they wish to accomplish in this unit. Setting personal goals is admirable and may be helpful for selected units of study. For further examples, four complete unit plans are in Chapter 4 of this book, and in each, a pre-assessment method has been planned.

Another way to plan for diagnostic assessment and then for differentiation is to use the Adjustable Learning Grid (see Figure 3.2). It helps organize and visualize what we know about students, reminds us where we want students to go next, and helps us plan diagnostic measures that give us data to use for differentiation. We fill out the first item (the standards basis) of the grid and then fill in Part A with data from what we currently know. In the third step, we design a pre-assessment to give us information about the gap. Finally, we develop a plan in Part B for meeting needs of various students.

In each step, there are separate columns for different groups of students. Some grids may have more or fewer columns depending on how teachers wish to think about those groups. Some teachers may need to add a column for English as a Second Language learners. There are several completed examples in the chapter on using Adjustable Learning Grids. Remember the basic purpose of pre-assessing is to aid the diagnostic thinking of a teacher and increase the accuracy of planning for diverse learners. To do this, we need to pre-assess the gap between what we currently know about students and the next performance assessment.

Designing Rapid Assessments

Previous written work, meaningful dialogue, demonstration/ observation, advanced organizers, and problem solving are among the

Figure 3.2 Adjustable Learning Grid

Standards-Based Content, Skill and/or Assessment:		
Pre-Assessment Tool or Method:		

	Filling In the Gap:	Filling In the Gap:	Filling In the Gap:
B			
	Concepts or Skills in Place:		
A		Concepts or Skills in Place:	
			Concepts or Skills in Place:
	High Degree	*Approaching*	*Beginning*

best methods of assessing the gap. Assessing the gap does not mean that we have a ton of extra grading to do or that it takes a lot of class time to complete. To create a rapid assessment, we can often use the first chunk of learning in a unit as a diagnostic tool or the first couple of homework assignments or small group interactions.

If we create a rapid pre-assessment with careful consideration of what we already know, the average assessment of the gap between where students are now and where they need to be at the end of the next unit should take about ten minutes. We call this a short form pre-assessment, and there are many ways to get information rapidly. Group discussions, individual or group demonstration of skills, use of a tool or technique, brainstorming, and other methods do not have to take much time. The key factor in the amount of time is the teacher's observation of the students for specific information. Pay attention to the purpose of the upcoming learning, the thinking depth, and the process or demonstration of skills required as well as the big ideas or concepts to be learned.

What are some efficient methods of recording and noting this information? Teachers can

- Take notes
- Have students complete a quick assignment
- Have students do a checklist with each other
- Use a ticket out
- Create a homework activity that helps gather data

There are many ways for teachers to take a little time and get a great deal of information they can use to plan how students will learn during the next portion of the unit.

Analyzing Diagnostic Data

Once we gather this data, how do we analyze it and then make choices based on the result? What should we analyze? Let's look at the characteristics shown in Figure 3.3.

Given the absence or presence of these characteristics, teachers can make informed decisions about how and what to teach next. This list may help us adjust the questions we ask, the time the next step in learning takes, the materials we use, and the methods the students use to communicate what they know and are able to do. Teachers can use their notes or short assignments from the pre-assessment to help think about flexible grouping, choices to give students, methods to approach new learning, and the amount of rehearsal that may be needed next.

What are some ways to use diagnostic data to adjust instruction and learning? There is no magic formula, but here are some ideas to help you think about next steps. This is followed by methods for meeting the needs

Figure 3.3 Analyzing Diagnostic Data

Areas for Analysis of Pre-Assessment or Diagnostic Data	What to Look for During a Pre-Assessment Opportunity
Concepts or content	• Incorrect assumptions or misinformation • Prerequisite concepts • Ability to use concepts in context • Ability to generalize • Ability to elaborate or extend explanation or examples • Ability to note a pattern or group in which the concept fits
Critical thinking	• Can formulate relevant questions about concept or process • Uses multiple methods or means to arrive at conclusions • Summarizes and states ideas in own words • Draws relevant or logical conclusions • Recognizes errors or misinformation • Finds ways to use concepts • Solves problems • Complexity of questions asked
Skill or process	• Developmental prerequisites to new learning • Current use of skill or process in part or whole • Willingness to guess, approximate, or attempt skill or process • Degree of understanding of the relevance between the concept and the skill or process • Degree of accuracy or self-evaluation of accuracy • Ability to use a model and/or rubric to improve own work

of diverse learners in each area of diagnostic assessment. There are more ideas in upcoming chapters as well.

Concepts and Content

To respond to variation in concept acquisition and use, a teacher may need to adjust the amount of time in a unit devoted to background information and to carefully select the best vocabulary acquisition method, given student needs and the desired learning. Select methods that allow students to attain clarity of concepts and the necessary depth of thinking about the concepts to best perform on the final assessment. Take a look at Nagy's (2000) ideas on vocabulary acquisition.

If you find that students or a group of students have a limited ability to generalize concepts in the unit or bring limited pre-skills, try a method called Semantic Feature Analysis (see Figure 3.4). This helps students establish context, patterns, and schema to understand complex ideas with clarity. Have the students develop a chart at the beginning of the unit. They can end each day or period by trying to fill out a bit more of the chart. When the unit is introduced, small groups can be assigned a chart or an area of the chart to work on.

A similar approach can be used with a progressive mind map of content and concepts. The mind map can be added to and used both as a pre-assessment and as a formative assessment source throughout the unit. It can be an individual or partner-based task. Many other visual representations and graphic or advanced organizers work well in teaching and attaining concepts. This is one of the easiest ways to differentiate instruction to the needs of diverse learners. Using advanced organizers has a high payoff in increasing student performance (Marzano, 2003). Students, especially those who are highly visual learners, can even design their own organizers.

Critical Thinking

Adjust your questioning and the context in which you teach the big concepts and process for the unit. In addition, adjust your groupings to better meet student needs for self-reflection and group processing. Larger group work (five or six students or whole group) works well at initial stages of learning and as students achieve the beginnings of clarity in thinking. Using individual rehearsal or placing students in pairs and triads works well as students attempt to attain deeper thinking skills. As students are ready to formulate more complex questions, they can work in larger groups, but they do so more effectively when they are given initial individual time to think and self-reflect. Take a look at Marzano's (2003) research on groups and group size. Also consider the work of Paul and Elder (2001) on critical thinking.

If you find students lack clarity, then try

- Adjusting your questions or giving them extra time to ask questions
- Having students put new ideas in their own words
- Having students draw a picture or give an example
- Asking students to do a journal entry to explain an idea

If students lack depth in thinking about issues and concepts in a unit, try using a method like Socratic Seminar or the Four Squares for Creativity method discussed next. Encouraging creative solutions or generalizing ideas to new circumstances helps students deepen their thinking.

Figure 3.4 Semantic Feature Analysis for a Unit About Freedom

Examples → Characteristics ↓	USA	Iran	Russia	North Korea
Personal rights of free speech				
Ability to vote				
Right to pursue all forms of work				
Right to worship in any way				
Right to nondiscrimination based on race, creed, or other				
Add other characteristics from your notes:				

Using Four Squares for Creativity. The teacher begins by posing a question or stating an issue. Then the students work in groups using Four Square charts (see the samples in Figures 3.5 and 3.6) during the middle of the unit to deepen their thinking significantly. When students get good at this, many can create their own Four Square projects. This works as well in history and science as it does in art or computer technology. The four essential elements of the Four Squares method are

- Fluency: generating many ideas
- Flexibility: shifting perspective easily
- Originality: conceiving of something new
- Elaboration: building on other ideas

Figure 3.5 Four Squares for Creativity: Secondary Example

Question: Why do some countries restrict the rights of citizens?

Generate as many ways to solve or answer the question as you can in five minutes. Use brainstorming rules. To control information To possess wealth To change government or laws To protect the citizens To adjust to a change in circumstances	In what other subjects or areas are these issues or questions relevant? Logical guesses are OK. (Our topic is the Bill of Rights) Terrorism War Economics Discrimination
Fluency	*Flexibility*
Originality	*Elaboration*
Think of a new way to state the question or issue. Write and draw ideas. *Is there ever a reason to justify the restriction of any rights of citizens?*	Take two or three of the ideas listed in the first square and explain them further. Give examples or write pros and cons of a solution listed, recording these on a T-Chart. *Protect citizens:* Pro: To reduce the possibility of a terrorist act Con: May go too far in restricting the rights of one group over another *Adjust to changed circumstances:* Pro: New regulations after a severe draught or economic down cycle may cause better prevention in the future Con: May be too little too late or may not have positive future impact, may result in multiple lawsuits

Figure 3.6 Four Squares for Creativity: Elementary Example

Question: What kind of pet is best?

List as many kinds of pets as you can in five minutes. Use brainstorming rules. Dog Cat Turtle Fish Hamster Snake	What kind of pets do you think your parents would like? You can guess. Dog Fish Turtle No pets
Fluency	*Flexibility*
Originality	*Elaboration*
Think of a way to talk your parents into letting you have a pet. Write and draw ideas. *Make promises to take care of the pet. Write and sign my promises.* 	List the reasons why the animal you listed would be a good pet and list why it would not. *Dog:* Good pet: friendly, likes to play, goes with me, likes other kids Not such a good pet: a lot of work to take care of like feeding, walking, and cleaning up *Snake:* Good pet: not everyone has a snake, easy to take care of some kinds, could live in a tank Not such a good pet: people are afraid of snakes, some might need live food, might get out of the tank

Ideas about grouping. Remember to adjust grouping throughout your unit to provide thinking opportunities in multiple contexts. While there are no hard-and-fast rules, a few reminders regarding grouping may help teachers plan differentiated strategies for student learning. Students with similar abilities or styles should be grouped only temporarily (Marzano, 2003). Use data driven, flexible grouping to achieve the best results. Do provide plenty of individual rehearsal when students are first trying to deepen their understanding. When trying to establish the needed initial clarity of thought, use partners or small groups. Complex application and integration of ideas can easily be done in groups of two and three, where no one can hide or miss out on participating.

Skill or Process

Self-evaluation level is a key component. You may need to extend rehearsal time or do multiple demonstrations before students can self-adapt the learning. Using models or modeling and a rubric or checklist makes a big difference in adjusting for diverse student needs. Younger students may do well with a simple checklist or a rubric using graphics or models. Older students may need the rubric broken down or "unwrapped" to help with self-evaluation. Take a look at the work of Reeves (2000) and Ainsworth (2003b) on using rubrics and models.

If students lack the prerequisite skills or are advanced in skills or processes, you may need to adjust the early methods of instruction in your unit. Methods such as menu-driven and tiered assignments work well in this circumstance. Offering students a choice or structuring a choice based on your pre-assessment data will help you accommodate multiple learners.

Try working with other teachers in your grade or content area as you develop these types of approaches. There is much benefit in a "divide and conquer" method to getting the planning done. Some effective menu-driven and center-based planning tips are found in Figures 3.7 and 3.8. Some of the tips may work better in elementary grades, and some may work more effectively in various middle school and high school content areas.

FORMATIVE ASSESSMENT

Becoming a diagnostic thinker means that we need to learn to use formative data early in a unit to make better choices about how we teach our students. The more accurate our choices, the more we increase the probability that a greater number of students will reach proficiency or higher levels of performance on the final assessment for the unit. There are many ways to group students, to base teaching on utilization concepts, and to employ effective strategies for deepening thinking in students. Those are good places to start adjusting our instruction and student learning.

Let us return to our earlier model of teachers as diagnostic assessors of students. Our goal as assessors is to determine current performance and potential. By looking at both the current skill level and the capacity to move forward, teachers can craft a learning environment that meets the diverse needs of students through a variety of methods. Once we assess the students at the start of the unit and carefully adjust learning for the beginning stages of the unit, what happens next? Are we finished assessing until the end of the unit? To continue the process of learning, we need to gather data at key points in the unit. Teachers need to analyze this formative data and continue to make course corrections so that more students will reach proficient performance by the end of the unit. Two major forces are at work as we assess students along the way; one tells us how to assess and the other when to assess.

Figure 3.7 Menu-Driven Planning Tips

1. Keep all options equal in terms of standards, rehearsal for the final assessment, and scoring

2. Develop scoring for the overall project that could be met with any of the options or develop a congruent checklist for each item on the menu

3. Keep all verbs at the application level or higher if menus are offered for assessment

4. Where possible, allow student choice if formative assessment indicates a similar experience level with the content or if the critical thinking level is not an issue

5. Do not allow student choice if prior data indicates difficulty with communication skills required on the final assessment or if the student has not demonstrated the critical thinking required on the final assessment

6. Use variety over time and units; menus should not be used for every assignment

Figure 3.8 Center-Based Planning Tips

1. Plan for the individual rehearsal of skills and thinking by creating rules or guidelines for each center

2. Models for centers help students who will be demonstrating, performing, or writing

3. Investigation and problem solving are important components of centers used for higher levels of critical thinking or assessment

4. Each center should be introduced to the whole group of students who will use it with visual and oral expectations

5. Centers should be clearly tied to the standards and not just be a place to go when your work is complete

6. Incorporation of technology is an excellent use of centers

7. Learning contracts or personal goals work well with center-based learning

8. Incorporate some form of student self-evaluation

Student Reflection

The first force or factor to consider is that multiple studies indicate student self-reflection and self-evaluation are among the clearest indicators of student formative performance. When we look at several studies, a pattern begins to emerge. In the British study on mathematics (Williams & Ryan, 2000), formative data collection revolved around the students' ability to describe why one problem was correct and another was flawed. This study determined that if a student could clearly understand and recognize errors, depth of thinking around mathematical concepts was evident. This study found that by valuing error detection and student explanation, teachers could easily determine whether the numeracy concepts were in place for the next steps of instruction and whether the needed adaptive reasoning was developing.

In an earlier work, teachers were coached on getting students to restate questions to refine their thinking in response to an incorrect answer (Orlich et al., 1980). Questions should be different in this situation. The teacher may ask

- How could you determine if your response is correct or incorrect?
- Could you work with a partner to list criteria by which to determine if this is correct or not?

Paul and Elder (2001) discuss the importance of questioning underlying assumptions based not only on topic but on the content taught. In each of the studies and works cited, the theme is having students determine where assumptions and errors may exist. We can use this information to help us determine how to construct formative assessments.

Curricular Transitions

The second major factor in formative assessment lies in the construction of curricula. Most curricula, especially standards-based curricula, are hierarchical. That is, concepts appear again and again in deeper and more complex forms as a student journeys through school. The key factor for assessment is the transition points within the increasing complexity of curricula. Transition points in learning are the points at which the skill load significantly increases and the critical thinking deepens or expands (Kuzmich, 1998).

Example 1: Math. Let us take an example in math and use both factors. The next chunk of learning will involve the complex use of the division algorithm to solve multistep problems. The step before that may include the numeracy and algorithm knowledge needed to understand division and to calculate accurately. This is a transition point in the unit. The teacher will need information about one step of skills before using that set of skills to move more deeply into adaptive reasoning and strategizing. At this point, we can give students two problems using division and other numeracy concepts, one done correctly and one done incorrectly. Students can analyze the problems and solutions to determine which one is in error and why, as well as which one is correct and why. This can be a class assignment with a partner, a homework assignment with a written analysis, or any other form that makes sense.

Example 2: Language Arts. Students are working through multiple stories in a unit built around a theme, era, or genre. Students will need to clearly understand point of view before moving to the next level of understanding, such as historical context or plot strategy. This is a transition point in the unit. A great way to assess point of view is to have students formulate questions to ask the author. Formulating questions is another excellent way for teachers to note students' thinking and progress in a unit. Having pairs of students share their questions with another pair (Pairs-Squared is a great technique) furthers the discussion and allows the teacher to listen for information, concepts, and thinking essential to this point in the unit. This helps the teacher to decide when to move forward.

Example 3: Music. In music, a unit on cultural influences may include pieces from certain time periods or artists. Before discussing cultural influences, we need to be able to hear differences in musical selections and develop criteria for describing the differences. Establishing these criteria is an excellent formative assessment for this transition point in learning. Students could work in groups to listen to pieces and develop descriptors or analogies for the music.

The teacher could ask

- How they arrived at those criteria
- What judgments they made
- What information they used

This process will give the music teacher a great deal of information about planning the next steps in learning.

Rubrics

In any unit and any content area, using models and exemplars with rubrics or scoring guides is another excellent method of formative assessment. At a transition point, students can correct their own work or that of a peer, using the models and rubrics to guide the process. The more students are able to self-evaluate and self-correct in this manner, the more likely they are to achieve at the proficient or higher level on the final assessment. In some subjects, for example, physical education, science, or music, the exemplar may be a demonstration or an audio or film clip, especially when students need to self-correct a technique.

Adjustable Assignments

Formative assessments give us information on how to

❑ Adjust our timing

❑ Plan rehearsal amount and materials

❑ Plan strategies for the next phase of the unit

We are still going to teach this, but perhaps different students will need more prompts or an organizer to help them think. Learners who have more experience or skill may need a different type of assignment, one that helps them expand their thinking. Chapter 5 on adjustable assignments and Chapter 6 on instructional strategies will give you many ideas for differentiating using this data.

In summary, transition points in a unit occur just before the skill level and thinking level increase substantially. At these points, teachers need information so that they can continue to adjust the accuracy of instruction and learning. There are many ways to focus formative assessments, but certain well-researched methods give teachers rich and in-depth information about what students know, understand, and can use.

Key methods in the formative assessment of students include

- Detecting errors and analyzing models
- Detecting assumptions
- Formulating questions
- Developing criteria
- Developing analogies
- Using models/exemplars and rubrics for students to correct their work

These types of formative assessments can be planned well ahead of time as the unit is being developed. These assessments are excellent forms of learning and can be part of regular assignments or homework. Data collection can take place individually or in a group, formally or informally. The key is to collect the data at transition points and to use what is learned to create choices and options for the next phase of the unit.

Collaborative Analysis of Student Work

Another area for formative and summative assessment data is the collaborative analysis of student work. Colleagues sitting down to look at and discuss student work, whether it is writing or other performance products, are practicing an essential form of assessment data collection. There are several ways to discuss student work and Web sites to support that endeavor, including those of the National Staff Development Council and the Midwest Regional Educational Lab. Many authors and speakers discuss student work analysis as well as lesson analysis as effective forms of data collection.

Two key factors in structuring this conversation have to do with the questions we ask and interrater reliability. Can two or more teachers agree that a given product or performance means the same level of achievement? What is the gap in learning for a particular student or group of students?

Can teachers agree on what the next steps should be to increase learning of students? This activity can be both formative and summative in terms of data gathering. It can be used to make better decisions about learning, and it can be used to improve rubrics and unit designs. The purpose of this type of analysis is to improve the accuracy of instructional strategy selection and increase the rate of progress for students. Figure 3.9 presents some questions we could ask about student work that may help us reach this goal.

Figure 3.9 Sample Questions for Reviewing Student Formative and Summative Work

---

- What percentage of students scored at each level? Which subgroups (learning disabled, gifted, minority) did better, and which did not? What adjustments did you or can you make for each group? How well did these strategies work? Which strategies would work best given these results?

- What was the level of critical thinking students demonstrated? Did it match the standards? Did it match the prompt and the rubric or scoring guide? Did you pre-assess for this? Did students receive instruction and learning opportunities at this level of thinking prior to the final assessment?

- What did the section or items of the assignment/assessment look like in terms of student performance? Do you have other evidence confirming that this is an accurate picture of students' level of performance?

- What might have caused these results? Look at time spent learning, resources used, strategies for both learning and instruction, and the goals of the unit or lesson.

This ongoing dialogue among professionals can truly change the nature of data gathering and analysis. It is always helpful and more efficient to have the perspective of other professionals. Collectively, our repertoire is greater than any individual's collection of strategies. Finding the key to learning for each student or group of students often requires more than one perspective. Asking good questions about learning, growth, and curriculum and then tying our next steps to making better decisions about strategies will have high payoffs for our learners.

FINAL ASSESSMENT

Using Data From the Final Assessment in One Unit to Plan the Next Unit

Data from student performance in one unit is valuable in helping make decisions for the next unit. We can use information about

- Student depth of understanding of the concepts
- Level of communication about what they know and can do
- Their ability to use these concepts to generalize or elaborate learning

This helps us adjust methods, materials, timing, and grouping to accommodate the learning styles and needs of diverse learners. One key factor that helps us garner usable information lies in the construction of the final assessment (Wiggins & McTighe, 1998).

In formulating a performance-based assessment, it is important to distinguish what goes in the directions and prompt from what goes in the rubric. The left side of the rubric should contain one of two things: critical questions for segments of the unit or the key concepts in the unit. The critical questions can be written based on the concepts, skill demonstrations, and thinking needed for that portion of the unit. For more information about critical questions or a description of key concepts, see Chapter 4 on curriculum.

Useful data. If the rubric and performance assessment are well designed and other teachers would get similar results when evaluating student work, then the data from that assessment will be useful. Taking time for teacher reflection on student work and final assessment construction and results is important, and several authors have highlighted this success factor (Reeves, 2000).

Cause and effect. Teachers need to think in terms of cause and effect when looking at summative data from unit performance assessments or at any summative assessments, including state tests. At least five causal factors involved in analyzing the data from final unit assessments help teachers make decisions about future instruction. The effect is the distribution of results.

The causes may lie in

- The teacher's use of resources and materials
- The teacher's expectations
- The use of time
- The use of strategies for both learning and teaching
- The skills of the teacher in knowing how to select the best strategies for different types of learners

Example: Assessment data for a science unit. What are some of the questions we could ask about the current unit? Figure 3.10 is an example of the kind of thinking that may reveal valuable information about a science unit. Depending on the answers to the questions in Figure 3.10, teachers could refine their planning for the next unit, paying attention to time, resources, strategies, expectations, teacher need for information or training, and other considerations. If the next unit is on using data and statistics in everyday situations, given the results and the answers to the questions,

Figure 3.10 Determining the Causes of Unit Assessment Results: Questions We Can Ask

Science Unit on Using Physics Every Day: _____

_____

3% of students scored at the advanced level, 65% were proficient, 17% were partially proficient, and 15 % were not proficient.

Resources	Teacher Expectations
1. Was student accuracy an issue? If so, were calculators used? 2. Are available classroom resources adequate to prepare students for the assessment?	1. What types of things did the teacher do to address the growth needs of higher-performing students? 2. How might the scoring guide or rubric have helped students succeed?
Strategies	*Time*
1. Did you give practice items to students in advance that were similar to those on the assessment? 2. Were instructional and learning strategies optimal given the formative and diagnostic data the teacher collected during the unit?	1. Can the nonproficient and partially proficient students take this assessment again? 2. Did the teacher have adequate time to prepare students for this assessment and provide enough rehearsal of skills and thinking?
Skills of the Teacher	*Other Considerations*
1. Is the teacher aware of ways to increase the percentage of students scoring at the advanced level? 2. What questions does the teacher have about these data?	1. What did the subgroup or item analysis show? 2. Were directions clear and were models provided with the rubric? 3. What was the result of student self-evaluation and self-reflection during the unit?

teachers may need to adjust their planning around what advanced learners need and how to increase partially proficient performers.

Student Self-Assessment

Student self-assessment and reflection on that assessment are important factors in creating a standards-based environment where the capacity to reach proficient or higher performance is maximized. Without reflecting on our own work and learning, we cannot truly be learners.

Extensive work on student self-reflection has been done. Paul and Elders (2001) talk about critical thinking and self-reflection, and Reeves (2000) discusses the use of rubrics and models in self-reflection. In addition,

Figure 3.11 Some Factors in Designing Student Self-Assessments

1. Make tools simple to use and understand, easily accessible, and not time-consuming

2. Use the information from student self-assessments to help you plan instruction and to communicate with parents; use self-assessments to prepare for a student-led parent conference

3. Plan to teach students how this assessment tool will be used

4. Document patterns of learning for classes, small groups, or individuals to note student needs and instructional adjustments

5. Use the concepts on which you based your critical questions to determine areas for self-assessment; you can also use process, product, or skill steps, such as spelling, scientific process, math steps, sequence, and so on

Use some of these self-assessments as feedback tools to give students ongoing and specific information about their progress or have students give each other feedback. This allows students to monitor and adjust their own learning (Kuzmich, 1998).

we have noted work in Great Britain (Williams & Ryan, 2000) and the national movement in math, science, and literacy. All of these areas of study have included resounding support of student self-evaluation and reflection.

Sam V. teaches seventh grade social studies and health. He frequently lists three or four success factors on the board for a homework assignment. He has students write the success factors on the back of a homework assignment. The teacher asks students to double-check their work by applying those factors when they complete the assignment and making adjustments so that their work demonstrates success. He also asks them to be ready to talk about it the next day.

When looking at homework, the teacher randomly calls on students to discuss not just the assignment but also the success factors. His questioning may involve how the success factors helped the student, or he may ask students to read aloud the portions of their work that illustrate each factor. Sam V. has combined clear expectations for grading with student self-reflection. This teacher finds more students reaching the goals for the assignment when he includes this process. See Figures 3.11 and 3.12 for tips on using student self-assessments.

ASSESSING OUR ASSESSMENTS

We have to deal with high-stakes assessments and state standards. That is a reality of current educational life. How can we ensure that we are

Figure 3.12 Ways to Create Student Self-Assessments

- Have students use models and rubrics to self-correct their work or improve it to the next level of proficiency

- Use journaling or short written analysis

- Complete a Plus-Delta Chart (Plus-Delta = what is going well and what could be improved); use a sticky note or note card

- Use a portfolio approach and have students explain their progress over time

- Create a checklist on a piece of paper to attach to an assignment or write the checklist at the top of an assignment

- Use the scoring guide and have students check off elements as they are completed or have a buddy/peer help check

- Have models available and have students record which level of proficiency they think their work most closely matches

- Write the criteria for self-assessment on the chalkboard or overhead and have students copy it, then use it to self-assess

- Have students develop an analogy that represents what they have learned

aligning our unit assessments with the "power" or most important standards and benchmarks? How do we know that our assessments give us the necessary information to make valuable decisions about advancing student learning with regard to high-stakes standards? We have been working on performance assessment design for a long time in many districts. Figure 3.13 offers our process for assessing your assessments.

If your final assessments are truly based on the most essential standards and benchmarks, you will certainly get better results. To find out whether your assessments are aligned with standards and benchmarks, you can use the technique we show here. It works well to see if existing assessments are truly aligned or to make a checklist when creating new assessments. The key to this technique is to start with the assessment and work backward to the benchmark. All three attributes must be present in a well-aligned standards-based assessment. If we believe that what we assess is what we get, then the stakes are very high in assuring that our final assessments are based on high-stakes standards and benchmarks or learning objectives.

Figure 3.13 The Red, White, and Blue Test for Standards-Based Final Assessments

---

1. Big Idea or Concept Check: *RED*

Looking at your assessment rubric, what big ideas, concepts, and key vocabulary words will students demonstrate when they take this assessment? What are the big ideas and concepts in the benchmarks, and do the two lists match? If not, this is a red light telling you to stop, since your assessment is not aligned with the benchmark. To fix an assessment, you change the nouns and descriptive adjectives that describe the ideas, concepts, and vocabulary words you want students to focus on in this performance task. List those concepts on the left side of your rubric in word or question form.

2. Critical Thinking: *WHITE*

In your assessment, you circle the verbs in your prompt and directions to students. Then circle the verbs in the standard/benchmarks you want students to demonstrate. Do the two lists match? Are the lists at least a partial match? You may not have all of the verbs in any single assessment. If the right verbs are not present, then raise a white flag (metaphorically) and surrender or abandon your current prompt and directions by at least changing the verbs. Better yet, change the critical questions students have to answer as well. You can also review your critical questions for the unit to determine whether they deepen thinking sufficiently for students to demonstrate the standards.

3. Product, Process, Skill Congruence: *BLUE*

Take a look at your overall assessment to determine what students must do to demonstrate the benchmark or standard. What product, process, or skill must they demonstrate? Go back to the benchmark and standards. Is the product, process, or skill a logical match for demonstrating learning? An example might be that the standard and benchmark require interpretation and questioning of assumptions, but your assessment is a multiple-choice test. Interpretation and questioning lends itself more to written, oral, or visual products or performances. If the skill, product, or process does not match the standard and benchmarks, then your assessment has turned BLUE and it is best to start over.

If all three of these pieces are in place, you have expertise at designing *standards-based* assessments!

SOURCE: Adapted from Kuzmich, 2002.

SUMMARY

There is a repetitive theme in good assessment practice that is characterized by teachers becoming more diagnostic in their thinking. It makes sense to pay attention to how students sound and interact and to what they produce. Using that information to make careful choices about how learning should proceed takes practice. Start by trying one or two of the ideas listed and differentiating a portion of a unit or a single skill demonstration. Repeated success will help teachers to go further and meet more students' needs more often. Remember that this is not about individualizing instruction and learning for most students; it is about planning accurately for instruction that helps more students reach proficient levels and using differentiation strategies that make sense, given the data.

4

Curriculum Approaches for Data Driven Instruction

CURRICULUM MAPPING AND DATA DRIVEN INSTRUCTION

Problem-based math has led to a difficult paradigm shift for many districts. In one Colorado district, teachers at the middle level learned new methods of teaching problem-based math using small groups of students engaged in solving complex problems. Soon after middle-level teachers were trained, high school teachers began learning these methods and curriculum.

Elementary assessment results in math were pretty good, so the curriculum and learning approaches were not adjusted. However, this district noted that at the middle level, around seventh or eighth grade, the scores fell off a cliff and continued downward at the high school level. The district leaders began to question the problem-based math approach even though research supported the path taken by these levels. In addition, district staff was baffled, since the words *problem solving* appear in each of the six Colorado standards, and the released items from the state math assessment were clearly problem based.

Classroom-based data also revealed issues with growth at the secondary level. When the state assessment data were disaggregated by standards and benchmarks, a different conclusion emerged. While the overall results at the elementary level were good, the highest areas of performance were in procedural math and initial numeracy comprehension. Scores for the higher levels of reasoning required in some of the standards, like probability and statistics, were not as good at all levels. The district discovered a compounded effect when the curriculum at the elementary level was not adjusted along with that of the middle and high school levels. Vertical articulation of curricula is a critical component of a standards-based environment, where data helps inform needed adjustments at all levels. This type of adjustment is usually done at the district level rather than the classroom level. We need vertical agreement across levels and horizontal alignment within a level on what it is we are teaching.

Other important components of curriculum mapping are sequence and the developmental difficulty of the expectations for student demonstration of the curriculum. Heidi Hayes Jacobs (1997) has done incredible work in this area.

The problem with curriculum is often the "Dusty Binder Effect." This happens when we create elaborate notebooks full of information about what we should teach. We hand this to new teachers or vaguely refer to the existence of such materials. Jacobs (1997) proposes a much more accessible version of curriculum mapping and even has a very usable electronic version of curriculum mapping, as do several companies now, so that the adjustments can easily be made by district level staff.

Alignment of assessments is another excellent feature of this process. Tying the standards and data analysis results of high-stakes assessments to the curriculum mapping process is essential. Such mapping can be done centrally so that teachers have a starting point for classroom-level planning.

The first level of classroom planning that allows for differentiation is the unit plan. A unit plan can involve a single content area, or it can integrate concepts and skills from several content areas. In this chapter, we have adapted curriculum mapping methods from a variety of sources to a classroom unit-planning method that lends itself to differentiation and adds some components to take into account formative data about students. In Chapter 6 on instructional strategies, we give you differentiated lesson plans that match these unit plans. This method of unit thinking makes further lesson planning easier and decisions about differentiation a habitual part of the planning process.

It is imperative that teachers think in terms of the unit plan before developing any lessons or activities. Unit planning helps teachers align the entire planning process toward student achievement on the final unit assessment. This process also keeps all of the planning congruent with the standards or grade-level benchmarks established by states and districts.

STANDARDS-BASED UNIT PLANNING: SAMPLE MATH UNIT ON DATA ANALYSIS AND PROBABILITY, "THE SURVEY SAYS . . . ," GRADES 3 TO 5

Standards and Benchmarks

Whether or not district curriculum guides and sequences are available, all unit plans start with standards and grade-level expectations. In each state or region, those grade-level or course expectations are called something different. In Ontario, Canada, they are called *expectations* and *indicators*; in Colorado, they are *standards* and *benchmarks*; and in other states, they are *learning expectations*. In this book, we will use the term *standards* for the large overriding or long-term goals set by government agencies, and we will use *benchmarks* or *expectations* to note developmentally (grade or course) specific requirements.

The first task is to decide which of the benchmarks or grade-level targets to hold students accountable for in a given unit. It is best not to use a laundry list but to select benchmarks that reflect what student learning must be at a proficient level. If you are selecting benchmarks or grade-level expectations across standards or content areas, limit the number to those that will be reflected in the final assessment.

For example, the U.S. national standards for math contain four standards for Data Analysis and Probability, and then each standard has one to six expectations for a grade-level range. If a teacher chooses all four standards for third through fifth grade, there are eleven expectations. Which of the expectations are being introduced, and which are recurring and may need to be assessed to a proficient level? Which of these expectations are peripheral to the unit? Teachers need to pick the expectations that will be assessed and be selective about the ones that are introduced in order to establish a true focus for the unit. We will offer specific examples of how to do this in the sample units throughout this chapter.

Unwrapping the Power Standards

Doug Reeves and Larry Ainsworth (Reeves, 2000) have influenced the thinking of many districts by talking about *power standards*. These are the standards that have the greatest impact on proficiency and growth at any given level. Using power standards and then "unwrapping" those standards to build the unit plan and final assessment for the unit are essential steps toward student growth and achievement (Ainsworth, 2003a). These steps in the planning are so critical to a student-centered standards-driven classroom that, without the focus, growth will be compromised. A teacher or group of teachers who merely list fifteen benchmarks or a series of numbers that indicate or stand for the expectations will not get the same result as those who are selective and focused.

Elementary and Secondary Approaches

There is a difference between elementary and secondary approaches to unit planning. Many elementary teachers, especially in the early grades, often list every reading or writing standard for each unit. Unit planning may not be routine at those grades since literacy skills are viewed as continuous progress subjects. However, many excellent primary teachers accelerate learning by choosing a theme or topic in which to embed the expectations for learning and assessment. We know from both brain research and many other fields that relevance and context are critical to higher levels of thought (Parry & Gregory, 2003). At all levels and content areas, it is easier to think about units of study if you review the standards and expectations and then determine a context in which to teach them.

Materials and Activities

We have long been trained to take a published series and use a scope and sequence in a sequential fashion, following teachers' guides. This was (or is) true at every level. These materials then became the de facto curriculum. In a standards-based and data driven world of student learning, this approach will not maximize student growth. A curriculum must be planned on the basis of standards and expectations. Published materials are resources to use in a unit but are not in fact the unit.

Some of us were trained to come up with engaging activities, given motivational issues and learning style concerns. In the initial stages of the standards-based movement, as some folks gave up teachers' guides, we may have overcorrected with what we thought were authentic tasks. However, a series of pleasant activities with or without a rubric does not constitute a unit plan or a meaningful assessment for that plan.

Supporting Differentiation

As we gain a larger body of evidence about student growth, concern grows that our reform efforts may not have the payoff we need, especially for certain populations. There are, however, pockets of growth around the world that can be investigated and replicated. We know that schools with aligned curriculum, careful and frequent assessment, and thoughtful planning and dialogue experience more growth than publisher-driven or activity-based curricula. Now, with a push toward subgroup growth, we must get far better at planning for differentiation as well. Our experience with resources and work with engaging activities will help us if we do some careful "up front" work that is selective with regard to student needs.

Unit planning must take into account district, local, or state expectations of learning for the grade level or course. A district may lay out the curriculum in the history of a country to include certain major events, people, places, government structures, and issues. At the early elementary level in reading, a certain degree of phonemic competency and comprehension may be expected along with knowing the parts of a story or focusing on a particular genre.

To start a unit plan, we need to know what we are expected to include in our plans and assessments. However, we must go back to the standards and benchmarks to truly see how these broad subject area requirements will be filtered. The benchmarks provide a lens that helps us focus the type of skill demonstrations we will need students to display over the course of the unit. We discussed how to create focus and limit the number of benchmarks based on what is required in the final unit assessment. We can talk of other smaller or implied skill demonstrations when we discuss lesson plans (Chapter 7).

Key Concepts

The next step is to determine the key concepts on which to base the demonstrations of learning. These concepts are the big ideas stated or implied in the standards and benchmarks, which answer the following question: What must students know and be able to do?

Let's look at an example in math, linking national standards (Figure 4.1) and key concepts (Figure 4.2). Without a context, we may try to cover all of the concepts listed in Figure 4.2, which is in fact only a partial list. Choosing a theme or context is necessary as the first step to focus a unit. This theme often depends on governmental requirements or the nature of the course. The next step may include marking or starring concepts on your brainstorm list that must be reflected in the final assessment for the unit, as indicated above.

Not all concepts are created equal, just as vocabulary words may differ in complexity. In history, the concepts for freedom, citizenship, and the act of voting are very different. For example,

• A third grade unit may include an awareness of voting as a cycle of events in local government.

• An eighth grade history unit may include an assessment that requires the demonstration or role-play of citizenship in two or more eras of U.S. history.

• A tenth grade unit assessment may have students develop a comparative analysis of the levels of freedom citizens experience across several regions, or they may research freedom as a motivating impulse across history.

Figure 4.1   Math Unit on Data Analysis and Probability, Grades 3 to 5: National
Standards

Standard 1. Instructional programs from pre-kindergarten through Grade 12 should enable all students to *formulate questions* that can be addressed with data and collect, organize, and display relevant data to answer them.

Expectations for Grades 3 to 5

- Design investigations to address questions and understand how data collection methods affect the nature of the data set

- Collect data using observations, surveys, and experiments

- Represent data using tables and graphs such as line plots, bar graphs, and line graphs

- Recognize the difference in representing categories and numerical data

Standard 2. Instructional programs from pre-kindergarten through Grade 12 should enable all students to *select and use* appropriate statistical methods to analyze data.

Expectations for Grades 3 to 5

- Describe the shape and important features of a set of data and compare related data sets, with an emphasis on how the data are distributed

- Use measures of center, focusing on the median, and understand what each does and does not indicate about the data set

- Compare different representations of the same data to evaluate how well each representation shows important aspects of the data

Standard 3. Instructional programs from pre-kindergarten through Grade 12 should enable all students to *develop and evaluate* inferences and predictions that are based on data.

Expectations for Grades 3 to 5

- Propose and justify conclusions and predictions that are based on data and design studies to further investigate the conclusions or predictions

Standard 4. Instructional programs from pre-kindergarten through Grade 12 should enable all students to *understand and apply* basic concepts of probability.

Expectations for Grades 3 to 5

- Describe events as likely or unlikely and discuss the degree of likelihood using such words as *certain, equally likely,* and *impossible*

- Predict the probability of outcomes of simple experiments and test the predictions

- Understand that the measure of the likelihood of an event can be represented by a number from 0 to 1

Figure 4.2 Math Unit on Data Analysis and Probability, Grades 3 to 5: Partial List of Key Concepts Linked to National Standards

Standard 1	Standard 2	Standard 3	Standard 4

Data collection
• Data
  relevant
  experiment
  survey
• Tables
• Graphs
  Line plot
  Bar graph
  Line graph
  Category
	Data shape
	Data features
	Statistical methods
	• Analyze
	  Measure
	  Center
	• Median
	• Compare
	  importance
	  of data
		Predict
		Infer
		Conclude
		Study
		• Investigate
		• Justify
			Certain
			Equally likely
			Impossible
			Test
			• Probability
			• Predict

Concepts can, therefore, be developmental. Another aspect of using key concepts might be the varying difficulties of the words and ideas; this may allow us to differentiate within a single unit. All students in eighth grade may be required to demonstrate analysis of freedom in the United States on the final unit assessment.

Groups may be formed to explore voting and citizenship practices as illustrations of freedom in certain countries or through specific eras and events:

1. The group working on voting may demonstrate less sophisticated analysis skills.

2. The group working on citizenship may be able to combine factors in an analysis.

3. Both groups are working on aspects of a bigger, more complex concept like freedom.

4. They can share information or use what they know from these smaller groups to complete the final assessment task.

When selecting key concepts, it is important to understand the level of complexity. More difficult concepts may provide the framework and categories for the simpler concepts. The challenging and thought-provoking concepts may help us create the final assessment, and simpler concepts may help build understanding throughout the chunks of learning within a unit.

Figure 4.3 Math Unit on Data Analysis and Probability, Grades 3 to 5: Developing Unit Skills Based on Key Concepts and National Standards

Key Concepts: What must students remember and be able to use, even after this unit?

Standard 1	Standard 2	Standard 3	Standard 4
• Data Tables • Graphs Line plot Bar graph Line graph	• Analyze • Median • Compare	• Investigate • Justify	• Probability • Predict

Unit Skills: How will students demonstrate they can use what they learned in a meaningful way?

Standard/Benchmark 1	Standard/Benchmark 2
1. Students will design investigations to address a question 2. Students will decide which data methods will give them the needed information	3. Students will represent data in two or more ways to help others understand and compare the data 4. Students will demonstrate the use of *median* and *mean* to understand and analyze data
Standard/Benchmark 3	Standard/Benchmark 4
5. Students will propose and justify a prediction based on data collection and interpretation	6. Students will predict the probability of a result and test the accuracy of that prediction

Unit Skills

When we plan a standards-based unit, skills are the demonstrations of student learning necessary to provide the rehearsal and learning for the final assessment, since most state and national standards are written at higher levels of critical thinking. Skills should contain verbs found in the expectations or benchmarks for the standards as well as verbs that allow learning demonstrations at initial stages of understanding.

Figure 4.3 offers an illustration of how we can take key concepts and embed them into the demonstration of skills for a unit on predicting preferences in fellow students. We have determined a context; we will limit the standard and grade range expectations through a focused approach to the concepts and assessment. The skills help us describe the level at which students will need to demonstrate these concepts.

Skills are not statements or objectives that denote the work of a single day. Skill statements help us divide the learning into chunks or unwrap the standard. Lesson plans can be created from one or more of these demonstrations of learning (Chapter 7). Instead of prescribing activities day by day, lesson plans give the amount of time or days needed to develop the background and rehearsal needed to demonstrate the skills. All of these skills will be needed for the final assessment in some form and to some degree. Now we need to develop that final assessment.

States and regional standards are often confusing to use in planning concepts and skill statements if you do not have them filtered by district curriculum mapping. In a state like Ohio, where each expectation is broken into numerous very small pieces of learning, we would take a different approach. The small pieces of learning may lend themselves to the lesson plan and the larger headings to the skills. Remember to base the skills on the long-term standards and midrange portion of the standard for learning in a unit plan. Shorter-range goals, indicators of learning, or benchmarks are best suited to lesson plans that are built around chunks of learning in a unit.

Relevance

Students need a personal connection to new learning. It helps them form complex schema and develop good skills in generalizing what they are learning for use with other applications. We need learning systems that are "driven by realistic problems and questions" (Silver, Strong, & Perini, 2000, p. 70). When we studied Madeline Hunter and Carol Cummings and the elements of effective instruction in the 1970s and beyond, we discovered that relevance is a powerful motivator. In addition, setting the stage for realistic connections helps to get students' minds more ready to accept new learning.

While we understand the need to build authenticity into assessment and learning practices, we must plan for this in the units. Figure 4.4 shows an example of relevance for our sample unit in math.

Establishing relevance can be as simple as using a school-to-life orientation with careers. It can also be done by using a prompt or activity that helps students show their application of skills in daily life. An excellent way to establish relevance is through the questions we ask and encourage students to ask as we engage in meaningful dialogue. Internet searches on almost any topic or set of skills to be taught yield many good ideas. Another source is the national Web site for a particular content area. Using literature and quotes also helps us establish relevance when we encourage imagination or help students see others engaging in the

Figure 4.4 Math Unit on Data Analysis and Probability, Grades 3 to 5: Establishing Relevance

Why must students learn this and what need is there for this learning across time and applications?

Students will need to know how to use, understand, and represent data in science, math, social studies, and economics. These are important technology literacy skills for the 21st century and certainly useful career skills. Students may understand the relevance by having to review data representations from various sections of the newspaper and from magazines. A few graphs on viewership from a television station's Web site may also provide relevancy. It is important that students see the everyday application of what they are about to learn. This review of graphs could provide an engaging small-group introduction to the unit.

---

concepts being taught. Meaningful learning is respectful and invites students to see the possibilities. Establishing relevance helps engage students in a bigger picture of the world and relates upcoming learning to their personal lives.

Unit Assessments

There are many books and articles on how to create authentic performance-based assessments. These are the best types for unit-level final assessments. Most of the literature on creating final assessments includes

- A well-written prompt and set of directions
- A rubric form of scoring
- Models or templates to assist the student in proficient performance

Wiggins and McTighe (1998), Stiggins (1997), Reeves (2000, 2003), and others describe in detail how to create standards-based final assessments. For our purposes on differentiation and data use, we have focused more on formative assessment since other resources exist for performance assessments.

The next step in unit planning is to create a simple description of the final assessment for your unit plan (see Figure 4.5). This will guide and focus your work regardless of the method of performance assessment you choose (Chapter 3). The final assessment will ask: What does the demonstration of learning for this unit look like? Following the assessment description, we will develop a prompt (Figure 4.6) and a rubric (Figure 4.7) that allows the demonstration of our standards-based skills and concepts.

When creating a final assessment, examples or models can be collected or developed. Remember to base your left-hand column on concepts, not

Figure 4.5 Math Unit on Data Analysis and Probability, Grades 3 to 5: Final Unit Assessment Description

---

Final Unit Assessment Description

Unit Title: The Survey Says . . .

Students will investigate the entertainment preferences of peers and staff. During this process, students will analyze and report the results of an investigation that is supported with data and select a method of reporting that demonstrates their use of data, prediction, and analysis. A rubric and set of directions will support student learning and assessment. *See rubric and directions for final assessments.*

Figure 4.6 Math Unit on Data Analysis and Probability, Grades 3 to 5: Final Unit Assessment Prompt

---

Final Unit Assessment Prompt

Unit Title: The Survey Says . . .

We are going to investigate what forms of entertainment students and staff prefer during their free time. You can choose what to survey about preferences people like. Please follow these steps:

1. Create a question that you will ask to gather information about preferences

2. Survey at least twenty-five students from several grades

3. Create a table and a graph to show your results

4. Summarize your results using median and mean to help your audience understand the results and these mathematical terms

5. Create a prediction about how the next twenty-five students may answer (use the same number of students from each grade as you used in your first survey)

6. Create another set of data displays

7. Now compare the results from both surveys and decide how accurate your Step 5 prediction was

8. Choose a method of sharing your data displays, prediction, and analysis. Make certain you use data to support your conclusions

9. Use the rubric to help you plan and think about your work

    Remember:
    - Use of correct grammar, usage, punctuation, and spelling is required in all parts of your work
    - You can use the computer to create your tables and graphs or you can neatly write and draw them

Figure 4.7 Math Unit on Data Analysis and Probability, Grades 3 to 5: Rubric

Key Concepts	Advanced	Proficient	Partially Proficient
1. Data in graphs and tables	Tables and graphs are easy to interpret and contain labels and data that clearly answer the question	Tables and graphs are accurate and labeled and clearly display important data	Tables and graphs have a title and are easy to read, and accurate
2. Median and Mean	Students use the median and mean to help them draw conclusions and make predictions	Students explain the median and mean result in their data interpretation	Students report the median and mean
3. Investigation process and questions	Students can explain the process they used and can develop interview questions that help them to create the analysis	Steps were followed and the interview questions developed helped students collect data	Steps were followed, and the interview questions make sense given the assignment
4. Predict and Justify	Students make predictions based on data and can justify their prediction using the first data collection step	Predictions make sense given the first data collection step	Predictions include elements (words) from the first set of data
5. Analysis and Sharing	Students describe why the data sets are similar or dissimilar and what may have caused that result Students share their conclusions such that peers use the mean and median to draw similar conclusions	Students compare the two sets of data and describe the accuracy of their prediction Students share this information such that peers draw a similar conclusion	Students describe the final data collection and whether or not it matched the prediction Students share this information clearly. Students share tables and graphs such that peers can check the accuracy of the data.

directions for the unit assessment or parts of the assessment. Examples of prompts and rubrics may be complex or simple depending on the grade level of your students. It is possible to differentiate the assessment without differentiating the rubric. This will help teachers stay aligned to grade-level or course expectations.

CRITICAL QUESTIONS FOR UNIT PLANNING

Critical Questions and Higher-Level Thinking

Questions are the cornerstone of increasing higher-level thinking. Linda Elder and Richard Paul (2002) indicate, "It is not possible to be a good thinker and a poor questioner" (p. 3). Questioning is a key component for both the teacher and the students in a standards-based, differentiated classroom. A two- or three-year-old drives a parent crazy with a multitude of questions, and the rate at which the questions are asked and the type of questions are in direct proportion to the knowledge the child acquires. Good readers actively construct meaning through unconscious questions they continually ask themselves (Healy, 1990). Creating a classroom where questioning is the routine method of learning is essential, given the challenging nature of most state and regional standards, let alone the lifelong impact of this positive habit of inquiry.

Rich and meaningful questions to guide a unit of learning create conditions for thinking that pervade the unit. Students will want to do more thinking when these strategies are used. Modeling this as a regular component of lessons and units tells students that such expectations are acceptable and encouraged. Rules for learning that make sense for adult and child learners (Kuzmich, 2002) include

1. What teachers ask is what they get.

2. What teachers choose to model is what they get.

3. What teachers spend time doing in class gets done.

4. What dialogue and discourse occurs in a classroom directly influences learning.

Critical questions differ from essential questions in only one way, and that is through the three key issues that they highlight for teachers. Unit plans are driven and focused through standards and final assessment, so the critical questions we ask about our unit planning (Figure 4.8) help us to determine if we have created effective essential questions for the unit's final assessment. This type of critical questioning formation distinguishes these questions from those that may guide formative learning in portions of the unit lessons. If districts or schools already use the term *essential questions,* that is fine. Just remember the three indicators for successful unit planning and critical questions detailed in Figure 4.8.

The composition of critical questions can be focused around key concepts, levels of thinking, and indicators of the skill, process, or demonstration of learning for the final assessment. These questions are not the prompt for the final assessment since prompts require far more detail to be effective.

Figure 4.8 Critical Questions About Effective Unit Planning

Yes	No	Are the unit questions at the deeper levels of thinking needed to truly demonstrate the standard?
Yes	No	Are the answers to the questions crucial to the demonstration of proficient learning in the unit?
Yes	No	Do students demonstrate the answers to the critical questions for the unit as a part of the final assessment?

Critical Questions and Brain Research

This approach to critical unit questions lends itself to differentiation throughout the unit and closely follows what we know from brain research and learning.

Chunks of skills from the unit plan can be introduced to the learning, which allows students to rehearse and demonstrate aspects and uses for the concepts in preparation for the final assessment or in the construction of portions of the unit. These chunks of learning should always be related back to the critical questions. Establishing a clear connection to the critical questions allows learners to make parts-to-whole relationships throughout the unit. Brain research from a variety of sources underscores the need to detect patterns in neuron development and to build the complex schema necessary for higher level thinking (Hart, 1993).

In addition, split-brain research tells us that we have an innate capacity to deal with parts and wholes simultaneously; only then can the brain make connections and interpretations necessary to learning and future utilization of that learning (Caine & Caine, 1991). "Good training and education recognize this, for instance by introducing natural 'global' projects and ideas from the beginning" (Caine & Caine, 1997, p. 106). For example, a kindergarten teacher may develop a critical question for a unit on retelling stories and understanding sequence in stories. How can you retell a story with a beginning, middle, and end? The teacher can chunk the unit into three or four parts such as retelling beginning, middle, and ending. When the teacher introduces the work on the concept of beginning, the teacher may say the following to a class or group: "Our question for the unit is, How can you retell a story with a beginning, middle, and end? Today, we are going to learn two ways to remember the beginning of the story. These tricks will help you when you retell the whole story."

Teachers need to help students see the connections to the whole at each step of the learning or invite students to make those connections themselves throughout the learning. Students must have time to reflect on and integrate these parts-to-whole relationships. This can be done through dialogue, written reflection, demonstrations of learning, and numerous other methods of reflective thinking.

Critical Questions and Differentiation

Critical questions should engage the learner. When students look only for the correct answer rather than for interesting questions, they are condemned to "live inside other men's discoveries" (Vail, 1989). Critical questions should also set forth possibilities and options. This allows learners to use new learning and rehearse with multiple strategies and interest pathways.

These types of questions allow us to build unit plans that include the flexibility of adjusting for learner readiness and needs, yet still help us hold all students accountable for the standards. It is not acceptable to modify and differentiate the standards unless the student has a special education or English as a second language plan that legally allows us to differentiate and accommodate the standards for an individual learner. The rest of the class must be held accountable for the same standard, concepts, and demonstrations of final learning. How we get there, with what resources, at what rate, and with what guidance and tools is another matter. Building in choices is also an integral part of unit planning and differentiation. Changing the standard is not an option, especially in a world of high-stakes assessments and subgroup growth.

Critical Questions, Standards, and Benchmarks

Some teachers find that it is easier to start with goal-type statements since it helps them move from daily objectives to using longer-term goals to enhance student thinking and learning. While this is a great step, it is helpful to move into creating meaningful and challenging questions to help define the final standards-based demonstration for the unit. "A critical thinker is often described as a person who can evaluate the quality of thinking used to solve problems" (Fogarty & Bellanca, 1993, p. 226).

Teachers in some districts and schools have been told by their principal or evaluator that they must tell the students what standard or benchmarks are the basis for the unit or lesson. While that is a practice that makes supervisors happy, it is not the best approach with students. In our story-retelling example, should the teacher have told the five-year-olds the standard: "Students will read and write for a variety of purposes" (Colorado Department of Education Web site)? Would sixteen-year-olds really benefit

Figure 4.9   Math Unit on Data Analysis and Probability, Grades 3 to 5: Critical Unit
Questions

**What questions will the students answer, if they are successful on the final
assessment?**

1. How can we use data to predict how people think about and choose preferences?

2. How does the collection and analysis of data increase the accuracy of our predictions?

---

from knowing we are working on benchmarks 5.6 through 5.22? A
compromise may include posting the standards and benchmarks and finding ways to use them in communicating with parents and students in
newsletters and unit plan summaries that could go home. These could help
parents and supervisors know you are holding the students accountable for
standards-based learning. Worthy questions, written at a developmentally
appropriate level, will do far more for student growth.

In Figure 4.9, we offer some possible examples of critical questions for
our sample math unit. Note that the words or ideas used in the critical
questions should be easy to trace back to the standards and benchmarks,
the key concepts, and the skill statements.

Another way to use this type of questioning when you are introducing
the unit is to engage learners in developing questions of their own. This is
an important feature of this process if we use a constructivist approach in
the unit design. Students could compare their questions to the ones the
teacher developed, and the rich reflection that could occur as a result
would certainly be impressive. There are numerous ways to activate learning through the carefully crafted use of critical questions and student formation of questions; these will be discussed in Chapters 5 and 6.

PRE-ASSESSING THE LEARNING
GAP FOR UNIT PLANNING

It is imperative to define what we know about our learners and what the
target for this unit looks like. Then we can determine what we don't know
about learners and pre-assess that gap in information. In a learning environment where performance assessments are the rule for unit planning, a
simple Form A and Form B for pre-assessment will not work well. We need
information about our learners so that we can create the right differentiation opportunities in the unit. We can gather this information in a variety

Figure 4.10   Math Unit on Data Analysis and Probability, Grades 3 to 5: Pre-Assessment Design

---

Part One: What do we already know about our math students?

We will have information about their written reflection in math, calculation accuracy, and ability to estimate and some idea of their ability to create simple graphs or tables.

Part Two: What do we need to know to get students to grow from where they are to the final assessment?

We need to know student understanding and interpretation of data and student ability to communicate at an analysis level using the language of math accurately.

A Way to Pre-Assess the Gap

Students will be given a table and graph that represent the same data. Partners will discuss the data and decide what conclusions they can draw from the information. Teacher will listen for

1. Understanding of the visual representations of data

2. Logical conclusions given the data

Students will "Quick Write" about their conclusions. (Quick Write in Math: topic sentence is the big understanding, next two to three sentences are the supporting detail for the big understanding, and last sentence is the rationale or why the conclusion makes sense.)

Teachers will not grade these paragraphs. Instead they will note whether the writing

1. Is logical given the prompt and supports the conclusion

2. Demonstrates the ability to express analysis through writing about math

Teachers will be able to teach the concepts as expressed, but adjust their coaching, time, order, difficulty level, and supporting resources to address these results.

---

of informal ways. Pre-assessment methods and diagnostic thinking are addressed extensively in Chapter 3. We need to learn to take what we discover and differentiate learning opportunities, timing, and materials to better and more accurately meet the needs of diverse learners. The diagnostic thinking that teachers employ to make continuous course corrections in a unit is essential to the success of learners. These course corrections or opportunities provide a great place in the unit for differentiation. The first opportunity comes early in the unit as we determine what we know about learners and what we need to know to get more of them to demonstrate proficient performance on the final assessment.

Figure 4.10 offers one example, but many more possibilities would work. Also, check out other ideas at the back of this chapter and throughout the remaining chapters. Remember to focus your gap analysis on concepts, thinking skills, and the type of demonstration of learning students will need to be successful on the final assessment. You can use your analysis of this data to create differentiation opportunities in grouping, teaching methods, and learning methods.

CHUNKING THE LEARNING

Chunking learning is not a new concept. Brain research and the psychology of learning have talked about the need to chunk new ideas to integrate, remember, and use these concepts (Healy, 1990). The ability to chunk learning more effectively for student growth is a skill that teachers will need to advance as they approach the type of standardized and data driven curriculum planning that is needed to accelerate student growth. We must move beyond the remedial thinking of older models for Title I, reading, and special education groups. Chunking learning by critical thinking level and skill load will help us maximize the limited amount of time we have with students.

Chunking a unit means to divide a topic of study into logical portions of learning that may be longer than one day or one period in time. To chunk a unit, we need to understand the necessary sequence and layering of learning that would best assist a learner to get ready for or perform proficiently on the final assessment.

Chunking a unit into ever increasing levels of meaning and usefulness works better to advance learning than daily lesson plans. A day or a period is an arbitrary unit of time. Learning, especially learning that may need to be differentiated, does not occur quite as conveniently as daily lesson planning would lead us to believe.

Chunking affects how we plan lessons to differentiate. Planning day by day is frequently inefficient and ineffective. It is better to plan standards-based units and then to plan by chunking the learning into key concepts and combinations of concepts that need to be taught. Determining the optimal sequence of these concepts is also essential. Performance and thinking can then be verified through ongoing formative assessment during and at the end of each chunk of learning in a unit. Some chunks will take only one day. However, if concepts are grouped and timed well, most chunks of a unit will take multiple days or even longer.

We need to establish the background needed for the early learning of what the concept means and how to use it; then we need to provide rehearsal opportunities that allow us to approximate what is needed for the final performance assessment. The last step in the plan should be a formative assessment that tells us whether the student has reached the desired level of critical thinking and use of the concept. If your final assessment is unwrapped and forms the chunks of your unit plan, this formative rehearsal can take various forms before you plan for the final

Figure 4.11 Math Unit on Data Analysis and Probability, Grades 3 to 5: Chunking or Outlining the Unit

---

How will teachers break up the unit into chunks of learning that represent various degrees of growing skill and thinking?

1. Activating learning for the total unit and developing a survey question

2. Learning about visual representations of data

3. Summarizing using median and mean

4. Predicting with data

5. Analyzing data results and sharing

---

demonstration of this segment of the unit (Ainsworth, 2003b). The formative data we collect in either method of unit planning lets us plan for further differentiation of the unit based on the student's level of thinking and use of the concepts and skills taught (Kuzmich, 1998).

One excellent benefit of unit chunking is that in a three-week unit, only five lessons may be needed, each lasting multiple days. For example, Figure 4.11 shows how we might chunk our sample math unit for its thinking and skill load of key concepts. While this form of unit planning takes getting used to and does take time, this method also reduces teacher preparation by changing daily lesson plans into multiday plans around a set of concepts. This may affect teacher evaluation and supervision expectations, so principals and district staff will need to adjust any teacher evaluation system that requires daily lesson plans. This method of planning is well worth it in terms of increased student achievement. Numerous examples of this type of chunking rather than just daily lesson planning are given in Chapter 7 of this book.

SUMMARY

This type of unit-based planning is a highly effective way of keeping the focus on standards and student achievement. This method allows teachers to take a curriculum and turn it into meaningful connections and critical thinking and use of concepts and skills. Planning for data collection right away also allows teachers to plan for differentiation to better meet the needs of learners. It also takes the old lesson planning to a new level and reduces the amount of daily paperwork needed. Using this type of approach to curriculum makes differentiation a natural part of thinking when planning and adjusting for diverse learners.

OTHER SAMPLE UNIT PLANS

THE WEATHER REPORTER, GRADES K TO 2

Standards/Benchmarks: Earth and Space Science—Weather

What must students learn?

(Please note that while science standards are listed, this unit could easily be integrated with reading, writing, math, and even arts standards.)

Standard 1 (Colorado/national). Students understand the processes of scientific investigation and design; conduct, communicate about, and evaluate such investigations.

Standard 4 (Colorado/national). Students know and understand the processes and interactions of Earth's systems and the structure and dynamics of Earth and other objects in space.

Standard 5 (Colorado/national). Students know and understand interrelationships among science, technology, and human activity and how they can affect the world.

Standard 6 (Colorado/national). Students understand that science involves a particular way of knowing and understand common connections among scientific disciplines.

Benchmarks

    1b Select and use simple devices to gather data related to an investigation.

    1c Use data based on observations.

    1d Communicate about investigations and explanations.

    4.2a Recognize that the sun is a principal source of Earth's heat and light.

    4.2b Recognize how our daily activities are affected by the weather.

    4.2c Describe existing weather conditions by collecting and recording weather data.

4.4c Recognize the characteristics of seasons.

5d Identify careers that use science and technology.

6c Identify observable patterns.

Key Concepts

What must students remember and be able to use, even after this unit?

Standard/Benchmark 1b, c, d	Standard/Benchmark 4.2 and 4.4
Thermometer Degrees Temperature	Sun Sunny Shady Daytime Nighttime Heat

Standard/Benchmark 5	Standard/Benchmark 6
Weather reporter	Seasons

Skills

How will students demonstrate they can utilize what they learned in a meaningful way?

Standard/Benchmark 1	Standard/Benchmark 4
1. Students use a digital thermometer and are able to "read" the temperature using the word *degrees*	3. Students compare the temperatures in sunny and shady places as well as daytime and nighttime temperatures
2. Students tell whether a temperature is cold or hot	4. Students explain why it is usually warmer during the day and identify the sun as the main source of heat and light

Standard/Benchmark 5	Standard/Benchmark 6
5. Students report the weather	6. Students describe the type of weather characteristics for each season

Relevance

*Why must students learn this, and what need
is there for this learning across time and applications?*

Students need to begin to see that we are part of many systems. Weather is a great way to do that in the early years of elementary school. Students can create personal connections to what they already know and learn new ways to describe the physical systems of the Earth and solar system in relationship to weather.

Give students the job of predicting tomorrow's weather. Ask them to watch the weather on TV tonight and see if their prediction matches the weather reported. Write down and draw what they know about the weather the next day. How well did they predict the weather? Describe ways they will learn to make more accurate predictions during this unit.

Final Assessment Description

What does the demonstration of learning for this unit look like?

Students use what they know about weather and seasons to create a way to report about the weather for each season.

Critical Unit Questions

*What questions will the students answer if
they are successful on the final assessment?*

1. Can you tell what the weather will be like during the winter, spring, summer, and fall?

2. Can you report how hot or cold it is today?

Pre-Assessment Design

Part One: What do we already know about our science students?

Students know and can describe what the weather is today in general terms. Students have some information about the seasons. Many students know that if the teacher says that it is 72 degrees outside, that is the temperature.

*Part Two: What do we need to know to get students to
grow from where they are to the final assessment?*

Do students know why temperatures and seasons change? Can students characterize the weather and what they would need to do in each season?

Ways to Pre-Assess the Gap

1. Discuss these two questions with students and note responses.

2. Read a book about the seasons as a class and make predictions about the weather.

Chunking or Outlining the Unit

How will teachers break up the unit into chunks of learning that represent various degrees of growing skill and thinking?

1. Temperature and thermometers

2. The sun and heat-shade contrasts and sunny places

3. What do we need to do when the weather changes?

4. Reporting the weather

5. The seasons in our area and the weather

Final Assessment: The Weather Reporter

1. Students will choose a way to report about the weather and seasons.

Some examples:

- Use a verbal report or newscast with notes and pictures.
- Create a computer-assisted report.
- Write with pictures.
- Make a game.
- Create a song.

2. Students will use what they know about temperature and weather for each season.

3. Students will need to use correct spelling, grammar, punctuation, and capitalization.

4. Students will need to describe or show how the sun affects weather in each season.

5. Students describe or show how they need to be prepared (dress, walk, activities) for each season.

Key Concepts	Advanced	Proficient	Partially Proficient
1. Thermometer, degree, temperature	Students can use a thermometer and write the temperature in degrees, creating a chart to tell the degree of hot or cold	Students read a thermometer and create a chart or graph to tell whether it is hot or cold	Students can tell if a temperature is hot or cold
2. Sun and heat, temperature changes	Students can describe how the sun helps make it warm or cold depending on the time of day and the amount of sunlight	Students can describe the difference in temperature between sunny and shady places and daytime and night-time temperatures	Students can tell if it is warm or cold depending on time of day and amount of sun
3. Weather reporting	Students report the weather using temperature descriptions and the sun to describe characteristics of the seasons	Students report the weather for each season using descriptions of the weather	Students report the weather for each season using pictures to show how the major weather looks
4. Seasons	Students can describe how to dress and what activities are special for each season	Students can tell how they need to dress or act in each season .	Students can tell how they need to dress for each season

Student Checklist (in student language)

- ❑ I can use a thermometer to tell temperature.
- ❑ I know about the sun and how it gets hot and cold.
- ❑ I can tell what kind of weather we have in the winter, spring, summer, and fall.
- ❑ I can tell what we should wear and do in winter, spring, summer, and fall.

DO YOU KNOW YOUR RIGHTS?
GRADES 5 TO 8

Standards/Benchmarks

What must students learn?

(Please note that while history and civics standards are listed, this unit could easily be integrated with reading and writing standards as well as the arts.)

History Standard 5 from Colorado State Standards

Standard 5. Students understand political institutions and theories that have developed over time.

Standard 5.1. Students understand how democratic ideas and institutions in the United States have developed, changed, and/or been maintained.

Benchmarks for Grades 5 to 8

    a. Explain the historical development of democratic governmental principles and institutions.
    b. Describe the basic ideas set forth in the Declaration of Independence, Articles of Confederation, Constitution, and Bill of Rights.
    c. Give examples of extensions of political and civil rights in U.S. history.

Key Concepts

What must students remember and be able to use, even after this unit?

Standard 5–5.1	*Benchmark b*
Democracy	Bill of Rights
Freedom	Constitution

Benchmark a	*Benchmark c*
Historical context	Rights
Amendments	Personal rights
Citizenship	Restriction or violation of rights

Skills

*How will students demonstrate they can
use what they learned in a meaningful way?*

Standard 5–5.1	*Benchmark b*
1. Students will compare governments with freedom as a core belief with those that are not based on democracy	4. Students will describe the rights granted in the Bill of Rights and describe the impact on their families

Benchmark a	*Benchmark c*
2. Students will explain the reasons for the Bill of Rights and how this critical document has changed over time	5. Students will give examples of the consequences and rationale of rights that are denied
3. Students will explain the implications for participating as citizens in the United States, given the Bill of Rights	6. Students will understand current events with relationship to the Bill of Rights and give examples of applications of the Bill of Rights today

Relevance

*Why must students learn this and what need
is there for this learning across time and applications?*

Since it is important for students to form a personal connection with the Bill of Rights, they first need to see the relevance of this critical document in everyday dealings and various aspects of our lives as U.S. citizens.

One way for a teacher to set the stage for this unit is to bring in the following:

- A school district job application or college application with a non-discrimination clause
- A copy of the Miranda rights (from the local police)
- A copy of a blank tax form
- A newspaper
- A ballot
- A church bulletin or notice

Students are given a summary copy of the Bill of Rights and split into small groups. Ask students to explain to the whole group which right corresponds to a particular document. In addition, ask if they can think of any other examples.

Final Assessment Description

What does the demonstration of learning for this unit look like?

Students will investigate the current relevance of the Bill of Rights using newspapers and other periodicals. Students will focus on civil rights as a major historical and current theme, events related to the Bill of Rights, and its interpretations for citizens of the United States. Students will write an essay to summarize their findings on a particular aspect of civil rights. Students will also have a choice of ways to present this learning using ideas from multiple intelligences.

Critical Unit Questions

What questions will the students answer
if they are successful on the final assessment?

1. How will you compare the reasons the Bill of Rights was drafted and the reasons it is still a powerful and influential document today?

2. Can you design a summary and examples of one of the rights in the Bill of Rights and describe the role of a particular historical movement or issue that played a role in development of those rights?

Pre-Assessment Design

Part One: What do we already know about our history students?

We have information from the previous unit on the Constitution, which includes an initial understanding of historical and governmental documents that are important today. We know they can write and look up information and comprehend the main idea in historical texts. They also have an initial understanding of legislation and its impact on their lives.

Part Two: What do we need to know to
get students to grow from where they are to the
final assessment so that more students reach proficiency?

We need to know what informal information students have about the Bill of Rights. We also need to know if they can understand examples of citizens' rights.

A Way to Pre-Assess the Gap

1. Students will brainstorm a list of what they know about the Bill of Rights independently (done on the first day of the unit). Teachers will

determine the degree of prior knowledge to judge how much time to spend on the introductory portions of the unit and determine methods for teaching background information.

2. Students will use a newspaper article and the Bill of Rights to see if they understand the current application of a right (done as a first assignment after an introduction to the unit).

3. Teachers will judge what rehearsal may be necessary in comparing rights to current interpretations and to what degree writing summaries of information will need to be included in the unit lessons.

Chunking or Outlining the Unit

*How will teachers break up the unit into chunks of
learning that represent various degrees of growing skill and thinking?*

1. The unit is activated through relevance and application to students' lives.

2. A sense of historical background and context is developed, including the concepts of freedom and citizenship. What were some of the influences that led to the Preamble and the first ten amendments?

3. Examples are used to explain current application of rights, including personal application.

4. How has the Bill of Rights changed over time and why? What is the past and current relationship of the Bill of Rights to the U.S. Constitution (tying current unit to previous unit)? What were some of the movements and violations of rights that led to amendments eleven through twenty-seven?

5. Students will explore documents from nondemocratic countries and compare them to the Bill of Rights, creating a visual framework of citizenship.

6. Groups of students will research an aspect of a movement or historical period to describe how and why the Bill of Rights changed and the impact of that change today.

7. Students will work on sharing what they have learned about the rights of citizens in the United States.

Final Assessment: Do You Know Your Rights?

Students will be able to answer the critical questions for this unit through a series of tasks that demonstrate their ability to interpret and apply the Bill of Rights. You are going to investigate and research one of the rights in the Bill of Rights.

Directions

1. Look up two or three rights that interest you on the Internet sites listed, and then choose one of the rights on which to focus your research. You may work with a partner or two or by yourself on the research phase of this assessment.

2. Research that right, how it came to be a part of the Bill of Rights and what meaning it has today.

   a. Why did you choose this right? How is it meaningful to you?
   b. What was the historical background?
   c. Who was involved in the events or issues that led to this right being added to the Bill of Rights and why was it added?
   d. What rights were violated or misused? Was the freedom of a set of citizens compromised and if so, how?
   e. What evidence is there that this right is still important to you and your family today? Give examples, please.
   f. What do you see as the most important aspect of this right and how should we keep from violating this right?

3. Individually write a paper that answers the questions in Step 2. Please include a title page and references. Remember that the writing standards apply to all written work in this class. Be certain to edit your work before turning it in. You may ask a friend to help you edit and review your work. Review the models posted and the checklist for good research-based writing.

4. Complete the self-evaluation form for your paper.

5. Decide how you will share your conclusions and the information that you discovered. You may work with others who researched the same right, or you may work alone. Use the multiple intelligences suggestion chart to help you choose an interesting way to describe what your right means to citizens today and what it means to you.

6. Check the rubric below to help you with your performance on this assessment.

Self and Peer Assessment Checklist for Research Paper on Rights

❑ Title page
❑ References listed properly

❑ Answered each question

❑ Edited

❑ Checked model

❑ Double-check your work by rating yourself on the rubric

Rubric for Final Assessment: Do You Know Your Rights?

Key Concepts	Advanced	Proficient	Partially Proficient
Using examples of application to student and other citizens today	Students describe in detail and give personal examples of why this right is essential today	Students describe and give examples of why this right is important today	Students describe the importance of this right
Understanding what influenced the history of a right becoming part of the Bill of Rights	Students describe what was going on in the country when the right was added to the Constitution in the Bill of Rights, and give examples of rights that were violated	Students give examples of violations of rights that led to the creation of or an addition to the Bill of Rights	Students tell why a right became part of the Bill of Rights
Protecting our rights today as citizens of the United States	Students use examples from current publications and government documents to explain how we protect this right today	Students use news-based examples to explain how courts, law enforcement, and other agencies protect this right of citizens today	Students use examples from the newspaper or Internet news sources to explain how this right is protected today
Describing the role of important leaders in creating change in our country	Students describe the actions and thinking of key leaders in a movement toward creating change or protecting rights in our country	Students describe the role of key leaders toward protecting citizens' freedoms	Students describe a key leader or author of a right
Sharing what you learned and how it affects you	Students help the audience to understand what the right means to them and to other citizens today	Students help the audience to understand what the right means to them today	Students help the audience understand the right

Peer and Teacher Checklist for Sharing Your Right

1. I understand that this right is important today because:

2. This right is important to me because:

3. This right is important to others because:

PERSUASIVE WRITING— CONVINCE ME! GRADES 9 TO 12

Standards/Benchmarks: Language Arts 9 to 12, Persuasive Writing

What must students learn?

Standard 2. Students write and speak for a variety of purposes and audiences.

2a Write a variety of genres such as essays that persuade

2b Organize writing so that it has an inviting introduction, a logical progression of ideas, and a purposeful conclusion

2c Use vivid and precise language appropriate to audience and purpose

2d Plan, draft, revise, and edit for a legible final copy

2e Write in format and voice appropriate to purpose and audience

2f Vary sentence structure and length to enhance meaning and fluency

2g Develop ideas and content with significant details, examples, and/or reasons to address a prompt

Standard 3. Students write and speak using conventional grammar, usage, sentence structure, punctuation, capitalization, and spelling.

3c Write in complete sentences

3d Use conventions correctly

3e Use conventional spelling

3f Use paragraphing correctly so that each paragraph is differentiated by indenting or blocking and includes one major, focused idea

Key Concepts

What must students remember and be able to use, even after this unit?

Standard 2	Standard 3
Persuade	Conventions
Voice	Format
Claim or position	Self-edit
Rationale	Peer edit
Sentence variety	
Word choice	

Skills

*How will students demonstrate they
can use what they learned in a meaningful way?*

Standard 2	Standard 3
1. Students will demonstrate effective persuasive writing in paragraphs and letters	4. Students will edit and improve their work using a rubric and models
2. Students will choose and research evidence as a point of view on a controversial issue	5. Students will use peer editing to gain an additional point of view about their work
3. Students will write in a compelling manner to persuade a specific audience	

Relevance

*Why must students learn this and what need
is there for this learning across time and applications?*

The teacher can pique interest in this unit by describing persuasive writing as a key trait that adults need. Students will be given a recent county tax brochure with directions on how to persuade county officials to lower property taxes from the estimated value. Students will brainstorm how they would go about making a persuasive argument to county officials. Students will be given an appraisal form and a comparables report from a realtor so that they can refine their ideas around evidence. Students will also discuss other circumstances in which adults use persuasive writing to get something done.

Final Assessment Description

What does the demonstration of learning for this unit look like?

Choose an issue you feel strongly about from a newspaper or magazine article, a news report, or other current events sources and write a persuasive researched paper to express your point of view. Be certain to add enough researched details to clarify your point of view and also point out issues for other points of view. Make certain that your sentence variety and word choice is compelling, so that your readers want to understand what you are saying and want to finish reading your letter. Also, make certain that readers see a clear connection between the evidence you presented and your conclusion. See the rubric and models to help you write this paper.

Critical Questions

What questions will the students answer
if they are successful on the final assessment?

1. How can I research and write to persuade others that I have a valid point of view?

2. How can I make my persuasive writing more compelling to my intended audience?

Pre-Assessment Design

Part One: What do we already know about our English students?

We have samples of writing from other units that indicate some degree of editing, word choice, and voice. We have no current examples of writing to persuade. Sentence fluency and variety appear limited for most of the class.

Part Two: What do we need to know to get students to
grow from where they are to proficient performance on the final assessment?

We need to know the students' ability to research and clearly communicate a point of view.

A Way to Pre-Assess the Gap

Students in your class also take history and have already written a short research-based paper. Check with the history teacher and other teachers about their impressions of student research ability. Another way to assess this is to use a beginning assignment in the unit to fine-tune your coaching around research. (See "Chunking the Unit".)

To check on initial persuasive writing skills, have students write a single paragraph to convince you to cancel tonight's homework assignment. Make certain to give students two to three minutes before turning this in for final editing. This will give you information on how much time to spend on various aspects of persuasive writing with this class and how much coaching is needed for various individuals.

Chunking or Outlining the Unit

How will teachers break up the unit into chunks
of learning that represent various degrees of growing skill and thinking?

1. Introduction to persuasive writing: Why do we need it? See relevance above

2. Reviewing the model and rubric

3. Learning the pieces of good persuasive writing and practicing the pieces

   a. Compelling introductions and conclusions, adding background
   b. Using evidence for and against a claim
   c. Occasion/position statements and other ways to state your point of view
   d. Voice, sentence variety, and word choice that help the reader

4. Choosing an issue and researching your point of view

5. Time for research and use of graphic organizer

6. Final assessment

Final Assessment: Convince Me!

Choose a current event or issue that portrays a controversial topic of interest to you personally. This could be a topic or issue about which you take a side, feel strongly, or are outraged by current events. Prepare a persuasive paper arguing for and against your point of view. Use primary and secondary source research techniques and cite your sources within your letter. Use the rubric on page 113 and models you received in class to help you edit and improve your letter.

Steps

1. Review the rubric and model as well as the tip sheets you received throughout this unit.

2. Use the advanced organizer for the assessment. Get approval from the teacher after completing the topic. Be prepared to share why this is a critical or important issue for you.

3. Briefly state your point of view.

4. Complete your research and list points you want to make for and against the claim. Keep a list of sources. Use quotation marks in wording to note exact quotation if you use the original wording of the author or source.

5. What is your conclusion? Does it match your original point of view? Have you changed your mind or confirmed your opinion?

6. What solutions do you see?

7. Review the rubric and models and then begin writing your letter.

8. Use self and peer editing prior to turning in your work.

Persuasive Writing Template

Student Name: Block/Period: Date:

State Your Topic in Terms of a Question:

State Your Point of View:

List evidence for your point of view and the sources for the evidence:

List the evidence against your point of view and the sources for the evidence:

Which evidence was the most persuasive for you?

Given the evidence you collected, what conclusion makes the most sense to you?

Rubric for Convince Me!

Key Concepts	Advanced	Proficient	Partially Proficient
Claim or point of view	Claim indicates what is controversial about this topic or issues and why it is critical to this student	Claim indicates why this issue is important to student	Claim is stated and issue is identified
Reasons for and against the claim	Claim uses researched information to support the claim and identify other points of view	Claim is well supported by the reasons for and reasons against; brings up other points of view	Reasons for and against are listed and related to the claim although a direct connection may not be apparent
Organization	Writing has a compelling and interesting introduction and conclusion that are clearly supported by evidence	Writing has a clear introduction and a logical conclusion that are supported by evidence	Writing has a beginning, a logical middle, and a conclusion such that the reader can infer the author's point of view
Word choice	Word choice convinces the reader of the emotions of the writer	Word choice is varied and suited to the theme	Word choice is suited to the theme.
Voice	Writing is compelling and seeks to influence a specific reader or audience	Writing is clearly geared to a specific audience or reader	Writing includes the author's point of view, but the reader or audience may be unclear
Sentence variety	Questions, sentences, and quotes support a convincing letter	Sentences are varied in length and type to add interest to the letter	Sentences are varied in length and type and may or may not add interest
Conventions and editing	Not applicable	Error-free writing is submitted	There are few errors, and they do not interfere with the meaning or readability of the letter
Research use and sources cited	Primary and secondary sources are used and quoted in the letter to help make a point clearer or more convincing	Primary and secondary sources are used and quoted in the letter	Primary and secondary sources are used and referred to in the letter

Unit Planning Grid

Unit Plan for: Subject: Grade:

Standards/Benchmarks: What should students know and be able to do?
Key Concepts: What must students remember and be able to use, even after this unit?
Skills: How will students demonstrate they can utilize what they learned in a meaningful way?
Relevance: Why must students learn this and what need is there for this learning across time and applications?
Final Assessment Description: What does the demonstration of learning for this unit look like?
Critical Unit Questions: The students will answer what questions, if they are successful on the final assessment?
Pre-Assessment Design: What do we already know about our science students? What do we need to know to get student growth from where they are to the final assessment?
Chunking or Outlining the Unit: How will teachers break up the unit into chunks of learning that represent various degrees of growing skill and thinking?
Next steps to finish unit planning: • Create the final Assessment Prompt and Rubric. Collect or create models. • Create Student self-assessment tool or checklist • Use a "Planning Grid" for each unit chunk after you pre-assess.

Adjustable Assignments for Differentiated Learning

5

> I know where I'm going
> But I'm not sure how I'll get there
> There are many roads to travel
> And places I might go along the way
> To enrich my journey
>
> —Gayle Gregory

OPTIONS FOR DIFFERENTIATED LEARNING

In many classrooms, teachers plan learning experiences that move all students through the curriculum using the same road and mode of transportation, regardless of the needs, readiness, interests, past experiences, and uniqueness of each traveler. When we take a trip, we may all be headed to the same destination, but there are many roads to get there and many ways to travel. The course of the journey often depends on the traveler's past experiences, expertise, independence, preferences, and interests. The length of the journey likewise may depend on the starting point, destination, and mode of transportation.

Through the pre-assessment process, teachers can discover what students know and are able to do based on identified standards. A student profile that has been built over time, based on data collected by the teacher and student self-awareness, is useful in making choices for learning activities. These data provide information that the teacher can use to make instructional decisions—being sure of the destination, the teacher can adjust the mode of transportation, the speed of travel, and the route. Adjusting learning and assignments helps teachers meet their learners where they are and challenge them to take the next steps in their journey. Adjusting assignments increases the chances of students being "in the groove," engaged in their learning, and motivated to continue to learn and to reach the targeted standard.

Box 5.1 Questions That Need to Be Considered by the Teacher

- What is the standard targeted in this unit and lesson?
- What would success look like? How will students demonstrate competency?
- What are the various ways to demonstrate success?
- What assessment tools will be needed?
- What do students already know?
- What can students do?
- What are the students interested in studying?
- What are students' strengths or needs or learning styles?
- What choices might I offer?

Through the pre-assessment process, we learn many things about our students. Whether we use more formal pre-assessments such as quizzes, inventories or surveys, performances, or demonstrations or more informal techniques such as KWL, Tickets Out, journal entries, or teacher observation, we are constantly gathering data about what students know, are able to do, or find interesting. We also realize that students are at many stages of the journey based on their past experiences. If we meet students where they are and provide what they need to continue their journey successfully, they have a greater chance of persevering and ultimately reaching the goal. This will hopefully create a sense of "relaxed alertness" and "flow" that will engage the learner appropriately and increase attention, efficacy, and learning.

ADJUSTABLE LEARNING GRIDS

Figure 5.1 shows the basic template for an adjustable learning grid. Part A shows what groups of students know and can do based on the pre-assessment data that the teacher has collected and analyzed. Part A doesn't represent the number of students in the group but rather the existing knowledge or competency level already present for that group of learners in relation to the identified standard. Part B shows what the students still need to learn to reach the standard.

Obviously, students in the Beginning group could be exposed to very little of the basic knowledge. They will need to be offered different learning opportunities than students in the High Degree of Mastery group, who will need to be further challenged rather than retaught concepts and skills in which they already demonstrate competence.

After collecting the data about students' basic knowledge and competency levels, the teacher can choose many roads so that all students have an opportunity to meet or surpass the standard. This in no way says that students must be grouped homogeneously as a result of the pre-assessment. Many configurations of partners and small groups could be used. Neither are these decisions about number or time.

Consider the sample unit plans introduced in Chapter 4, along with Figures 5.2 through 5.5, which show how adjustable grids may be developed for those units. In each grid, Part B shows what still needs to be learned or accomplished by each group of students, whether Beginning or Approaching Mastery or at a High Degree of Mastery. When an adjustable learning grid has been completed, teachers may want to group the students based on their readiness and then keep them in homogeneous groups. That is an option, but it is certainly not the only option and may not be the right option in every case. If it were the only option, then we would be suggesting that tracking is better for students, and we know that this is not so. Groups can be designed in a variety of ways, as we will see in the following pages. The use of creative planning and flexible grouping is based on sound data and on knowledge about the needs, capabilities, personalities, learning styles, and interests of the students. Creativity and flexibility provide novelty and variety both for students and for the teacher and can be used to adjust many aspects of the lesson beyond ability or readiness levels.

ADJUSTABLE LEARNING ELEMENTS

When teachers plan any lesson, variables can be adjusted to meet the needs of the diverse learners in the classroom. Some of the adjustments

Figure 5.1   Adjustable Learning Grid to Record Data About Student Readiness Levels

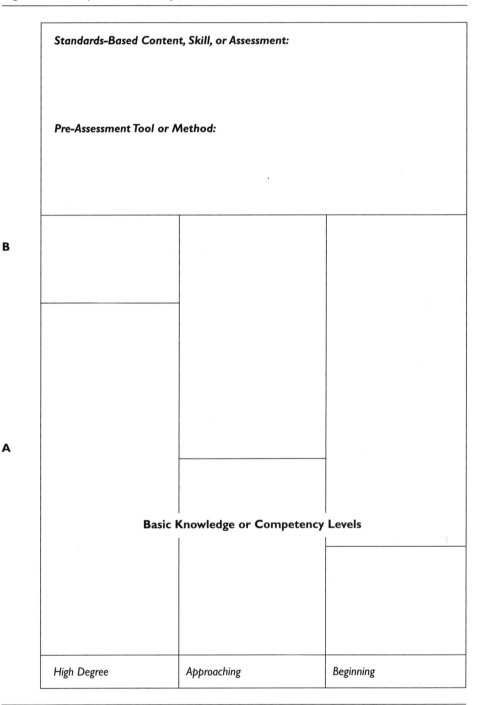

Figure 5.2   Adjustable Learning Grid for Sample Unit, The Weather Reporter, Grades K to 2: Record Degree of Competence, Not Number of Students

---

Standards-Based Content, Skill, or Assessment:

Students know and understand interrelationships among science, technology, and human activity and how they can affect the world.

Physical science: Weather and its impact

Pre-Assessment Tool or Method:

1.   Discuss these two questions with students and note responses.

2.   Read a book about the seasons as a class and make predictions about the weather.

B Plan for daily living and activities based on weather	Extend their list of characteristics of the seasons Predict impact of weather on daily living	Need to be able to name the seasons and characteristics Recognize the connections between weather and daily living
A Can name and describe seasons Correlate weather with activities and clothing needs Describe impact of seasons on daily living	List the seasons and some characteristics of each Correlate weather with activities and clothing needs	Describe personal physical reaction to weather "I had to put a jacket on" "I was so hot I was thirsty" When prompted could give a characteristic of a season
High Degree	*Approaching*	*Beginning*

Figure 5.3 Adjustable Learning Grid for Sample Math Unit "The Survey Says . . . ," Grades 3 to 5: Record Degree of Competence, Not Number of Students

---

Standards-Based Content, Skill or Assessment: Grade 3–5 Mathematics

Data Analysis and Probability: Develop and evaluate inferences and predictions that are based on data

Pre-Assessment Tool or Method:

Have students examine a variety of graphs and charts and predict and interpret data. Quick write (topic sentence and supporting detail and rationale)

B	Require complex data and challenging predictions that are relevant to their lives	Opportunities to collect, organize, and predict from data in a variety of situations	Beginning with simple data collection Provide a variety of ways to organize data Practice in making simple predictions
A	Quite capable of interpreting data and also organizing and recording in a variety of forms Understands averages Can analyze and summarize data to make predictions	Is able to understand and interpret data Can organize simple data in limited ways Limited predictions can be made from data	Has little experience with understanding and interpreting data Not able to define median and mean
	High Degree	*Approaching*	*Beginning*

---

listed below may already be done on a daily basis—often randomly and unconsciously—yet they still need to be considered in the overall planning process.

• *Differentiating content/materials.* Sometimes, students will exhibit a particular interest in some aspects of the unit of study and will want to go deeper into this area. For example, in a unit on the American Revolution, students may be interested in different individuals who had an impact or major role. Whether they investigate Thomas Jefferson or Paul Revere, students can still arrive at an understanding of the beliefs of a freedom fighter and learn about such concepts as fascism or democracy. Reading materials may also be differentiated based on the needs of the students, who may want to access a variety of materials and resources, from books to the Internet. DCM

Figure 5.4 Adjustable Learning Grid for Sample Unit, Do You Know Your Rights?, Grades 5 to 8: Record Degree of Competence, Not Number of Students

Standards-Based Content, Skill, or Assessment: Grades 5 to 8		
Students are able to describe the basic ideas set forth in the Declaration of Independence, Constitution, and Bill of Rights		
Pre-Assessment Tool or Method:		
A Ticket Out can be filled in by students, asking them to explain their understanding of the Bill of Rights		

B / A	Impact	Historical foundation	What is it?
B		Current personal tie	Learn basic elements of the Bill
	Knowledgeable about the Declaration of Independence, Constitution, and the Bill of Rights and their impact		How might it help us today?
A		Know some aspects of the Bill but not its significance	
			Students are aware of the term *Bill of Rights* but not its impact or content
	High Degree	*Approaching*	*Beginning*

• *Differentiating communication/technology.* Students may select from a variety of communication methods, from role-play to essay to presentation, depending on their needs or their interests. Technology may be integrated based on students' needs or expertise. **DCT**

• *Differentiating multiple intelligences.* Projects, centers, or problem-based learning activities may be created to reflect the different multiple intelligences. This allows students to find a comfort area, an area of strength, or perhaps an area that needs attention and bolstering. **DMI**

• *Differentiating readiness.* Students may be grouped by readiness or sometimes ability to deal with a learning situation that is just beyond their level of expertise. **DR**

• *Differentiating interest/choice.* Students are allowed to choose an assignment based on their interests or choice. Contracts, projects, and tic-tac-toe boards are useful in facilitating this. **DIC**

Figure 5.5   Adjustable Learning Grid for Sample Unit, Persuasive Writing—Convince Me!, Grades 9 to 12: Record Degree of Competence, Not Number of Students

---

Standards-Based Content, Skill, or Assessment: Grades 9 to 12

Students write and speak for a variety of purposes and audiences

Pre-Assessment Tool or Method:

Students examine previously written materials (perhaps from a portfolio collection). Students pair up and discuss strengths and weaknesses of their work (based on rubric) and identify areas to focus on for improvement.

	High Degree	Approaching	Beginning
B	Continue to work on creativity and ability to write and deliver powerful persuasive arguments grounded in fact and point of view	• Continued practice with the writing process • Vocabulary development of persuasive language • Identify conventions that need work and review and rehearse	• Review the writing process • Practice in organizing ideas and developing a persuasive argument • Review of appropriate conventions
A	Able to apply the writing process of developing ideas and content to persuade and compel others to their point of view Uses conventions appropriately	Understands the process of writing and is working toward mastery. Persuasive language and building a progressive argument not always evident. Not all conventions adhered to	Has difficulty developing progression of ideas and clearly stating point of view. Limited language of persuasion. Many areas of convention are lacking

---

• *Differentiating process.* Students may use different methods to process information. Activities are varied and engaging so that information and skills are rehearsed and applied in a variety of ways to increase retention and understanding.   DP

Although we consider these ways of differentiating in day-to-day planning, we also may see opportunities within the final assessment. In the final assessment prompt for the sample unit on "The Survey Says . . . ," for example, examples of differentiation are also evident (see Figure 5.6).

FLEXIBLE GROUPING

Based on the adjustable learning grid, we can make informed decisions about grouping students. We can respond to the pre-assessment data we

Figure 5.6 Final Assessment Prompt for the Sample Unit, "The Survey Says . . ."

We are going to investigate what forms of entertainment students and staff prefer during their free time. You can choose what to survey about preferences people like. Please follow these steps:

1. Create a question that you will ask to gather information about preferences (Differentiating Content/Materials) DCM

2. You will need to survey at least twenty-five students from several grades

3. Then you will need to create a table and a graph to show your results (Differentiating Process) DP

4. Summarize your results using median and mean to help you summarize the results

5. Create a prediction about how the next twenty-five students may answer (use the same number of students from each grade as you did in your first survey)

6. Create another set of data displays (Differentiating Process) DP

7. Now compare the results from both surveys and decide how accurate your Step 5 prediction was

8. Choose a method of sharing your data displays, prediction, and analysis. Be certain to make certain you use data to support your conclusions (Differentiating With Multiple Intelligences) DMI

9. Use the rubric to help you plan and think about your work

Remember:

1. Use of correct grammar, usage, punctuation, and spelling is required in all parts of your work

2. You can use the computer to create your tables and graphs, or you can neatly write and draw them

have collected in a variety of ways, rather than just leaving the students in three homogeneous groups based on knowledge and skills.

There may be some information that we want the total group to learn. This information may be delivered in lecturette, video, jigsaw, or other format. But we also know from the research on critical thinking (Paul & Elder, 2001) that for information to become knowledge, students need to process it independently to clarify their own thinking and to make meaning. Thus the next step should be an opportunity to discuss, explain, clarify, and question their thinking, perhaps by using a small group or partner format like "Think, Pair, Share."

The decisions about groups and group size are made by the teacher considering the

- Information sources available
- Tasks
- Student interests
- Skill or ability level of students
- Learning styles and multiple intelligences
- Thinking skills
- Process or product desired

Grouping decisions also depend on the creativity of the teacher in relation to student needs and targeted outcomes. The reality is that in any unit of study, some time must be spent in each of the areas that are defined by the term TAPS: total group (T), alone (A), in partners (P), and in small groups (S).

- **(T) Total group.** There may be information and new skills that need to be shared or demonstrated to the whole class.

- **(A) Alone.** Students sometimes need to practice by working alone, which is how they will perform on standardized tests. In life, we often work and think independently of others.

- **(P) Partners.** Partnering gives students a narrow audience with whom to share ideas, discuss new information, or process learning. This can be accomplished by random partners or teacher-constructed dyads.

- **(S) Small groups.** Groups of three or four students may be constructed for a variety of purposes. In any group larger than three or four, some students may be off-task or lack real commitment to the goal.

Teachers can use several types of flexible groupings, including

- *Ability.* Usually homogeneous based on needs
- *Heterogeneous.* Cooperative group learning

Figure 5.7 Using TAPS: Total Group, Alone, Partners, or Small Groups

TOTAL Whole class instruction All students doing the same thing	Pre-assessment Presenting new information Modeling new skills Guest speaker Viewing a video Using a jigsaw strategy Guest speaker Textbook(s) assignment
ALONE All students working alone may have a variety of tasks based on interest or readiness	Pre-assessment Journal entry Portfolio assessing Self-assessment Independent study Note taking and summarizing Reflection Tickets out
PAIRED All students have a partner Random selection (card, color, etc.) Teacher selection Students choose a partner Task or interest oriented	Brainstorming Checking homework Checking for understanding Processing information Peer editing Peer evaluation Researching Interest in similar topic Planning for homework
SMALL GROUPS Homogeneous for skill development Heterogeneous for cooperative groups Random or structured by teacher or students Interest or task oriented	Problem solving Group projects Learning centers Cooperative group learning assignments Portfolio conferences Group investigation Carousel brainstorming Graffiti brainstorming

- *Random.* Just to group quickly
- *Structured.* Based on students' profiles and complementary strengths and needs
- *Interests.* In response to choices and tasks that connect with learners or pique their curiosity.

Figure 5.7 suggests a variety of uses for each of the TAPS configurations, whether total group, alone, partners, or small groups.

DIFFERENTIATING PAIRS

Random Partners

Random partners can be used as a quick way to give students an opportunity to process information. They can be used

- To give students "airtime"
- To brainstorm or to open mental files
- To check for understanding of a concept
- To react to or rehearse new information
- To practice a skill
- To reflect on material
- To predict or elicit reaction, for example, in peer coaching or editing

Choosing random partners may be done as easily as asking students to get a partner who is physically near to them, or it may be facilitated by techniques such as appointment cards, with room for six or eight different appointments (see Figure 5.8).

To use appointment cards, students form two lines facing each other. The students write their names on the cards of the students who are facing them. Then one line moves one person over as in musical chairs, and the next appointment is made with the new partner. This process ensures that everyone gets partners and no one is hurt through being rejected. It is important in any classroom—not just the differentiated classroom—that all students feel included and respected.

Cards may be used with icons pertaining to specific units of study; for example, Figure 5.9 shows a fitness unit that might also include partners for hiking, tennis, in-line skating, or skiing (see also "Check Mate" in Chapter 6). In a unit on insects, students could make appointments with their

- Butterfly partner
- Housefly partner
- Ant partner
- Grasshopper partner

Or in a unit on explorers, students could make appointments to "meet with"

- Columbus
- Magellan
- Cortez
- La Salle
- Ponce de Leon

Figure 5.8 Appointment Card for Student Partners

Appointments:

1 o'clock _____

2 o'clock _____

3 o'clock _____

4 o'clock _____

5 o'clock _____

6 o'clock _____

Figure 5.9 Sample Appointment Card for Student Fitness Partners

Fitness Partners

Runner _____

Baseball player _____

Climber _____

Skater _____

Swimmer _____

Basketball player _____

Other _____

Random partners and random groups are often less stressful for students who are nervous about being left out. Students need to get to know each other and to value opinions from students within a diverse classroom group. These kinds of partners and groups also give students the opportunity to discuss, dialogue, and debate, opportunities that they don't often get in front of screens, whether television or computer (see Levine, 2002).

Constructed Pairs

Teachers often have specific reasons for partnering students based on their learning styles, multiple intelligences, interests, needs, or readiness. Teachers can consider the following ways to construct pairs:

- *Reading levels.* Students may be partnered for reading content from texts or articles, using recording or graphic organizers to help them capture key ideas or information that needs to be retained for use or discussion.

- *Complementary learning styles.* Teachers might want to match a Clipboard and a Beach Ball, for example, so that their innate tendencies are complementary.

- *Multiple intelligences.* Knowing the learners allows teachers to pair one student with a strong verbal/linguistic intelligence with another student with less strength in verbal/linguistic intelligence. Or a student with strong visual/spatial intelligence and one with strong interpersonal intelligence could be a good combination as they use their strengths, discuss their ideas, and reflect on their learning as a result of their interaction.

DIFFERENTIATING SMALL GROUPS

Group Size

In terms of group size, we need to recognize that less is more. Johnson and Johnson (1991) point out that it is hard to get left out of a pair, and most teachers who are beginning to use interactive strategies tend to focus on dyads exclusively, recognizing that limited interaction creates more on-task behavior and causes fewer conflicts and personality clashes. Students also may have difficulty working with others if they don't yet have adequate social skills (see "Cooperative Group Learning" in Chapter 6).

According to the research of Lou and colleagues (1996), small groups of three or four students are more productive than groups of greater numbers. If groups are larger than three or four, students may become social or disruptive loafers as they perceive that the learning task can be accomplished without them. Smaller groups also ensure that each student has enough meaningful work to do and make it easier to incorporate individual accountability, which increases the chances that students will attend to the learning no matter what the group size.

Ability Groups

These are generally structured based on student needs as a result of gaps in knowledge or skills determined by the teacher during the pre-assessment process or in day-to-day observation. Ability grouping should not be done on a permanent basis—to suggest the notion of penguins, ducks, and eagles—but for short sessions or brief periods of time to scaffold learning or to fill in a gap in the students' repertoire.

Research suggests that ability grouping should be done only judiciously and sparingly. Studies (Lou et al., 1996) have shown

- Low-ability learners actually perform worse when they are placed in homogeneous groupings.
- Average ability learners benefit most from homogeneous groups.
- High-ability learners have limited growth when they work together.

This is not to suggest that students should be tracked and left in these "ruts" but rather that they should be moved flexibly in and out of groups as required, whether the groups are homogeneous or heterogeneous.

For example, one teacher noticed that several students didn't seem to be able to log on to an Internet site independently. At the beginning of the next period, she provided three focus activities at the computers. She handed students a card of instructions as they entered the room. More advanced students were given a complicated computer search task. Students with average techniques on the computer were given a scavenger hunt. Students who needed more instruction and practice were in a group that was given a period of time with teacher support to review the process and thus were more able to continue their research.

Conversely, the teacher could have used a strategy involving heterogeneous groups of three, where students of three levels of ability worked together to collectively increase their skills and compete in a scavenger hunt against other groups. The judgment of the teacher and the decisions she or he would make should always be based on the needs of the students and knowledge that the teacher has about them.

Students don't all learn in the same way with the same timeline. They are also not at the same level in every subject area or with every topic. Each of us has areas of strength and competence, and conversely, each of us has areas where we need more growth. We differ based on our experiences throughout life's journey, and we are not always penguins or eagles in everything.

Heterogeneous Groups

Compared to homogeneous groups, heterogeneous groups are more effective in increasing performance, as noted in the research of Lou et al. (1996), especially for low-ability students. Heterogeneous groups may be formed by constructing small groups from a mixture of students considering gender, ethnicity, socioeconomic background, and level of ability.

Random Groups

Students may be grouped randomly for a variety of tasks that don't require specific structure. Of course, this randomness may cause some groups to be inadvertently homogeneous, with students who all are strong personalities, weak readers, lacking leadership skills, and so on. Yet in the real world, this also may occur. Thus we would not use random grouping for tasks involving long-term working relationships, but they would work well for things like pre-assessment, brainstorming, or examination of new information. To increase the true heterogeneity of the groups, the teacher may want to structure projects or problem-solving groups.

So even with random groups, teachers still need to proceed carefully, using their knowledge of the students and the tasks involved. Some of the techniques for random grouping include

- *Numbering off.* Divide the number of students in the class by the number of members that you want in each group. For example, if there were thirty-two students in the class and you wanted four in each group, you would have eight groups. Have the students count off one to eight. Then invite all the ones, twos, threes, fours, and so on to form groups of four and move to the assigned workstation.

- *Cards.* Often, teachers distribute cards with stickers or numbers on them. Students are asked to find two other students whose cards match theirs and form a group. In math, the cards may have an equation that equals a certain number. After students solve their equation, they find two other students who have the same math answer. Cards may have shapes or colors that need to be matched.

- *Line up.* Teachers can ask students to line up around the room in order by birthday (month, day) and then group them off in twos, threes, or fours.

- *Candy.* A variety of wrapped candy may be distributed, one piece to each student. Teachers may ask students to group by like candies or make a group with three or four different candies. (Note: Ask them not to eat the candy until after the groups are formed.) Students love novelty and respond to interesting grouping activities.

Constructed Groups

Students may be grouped according to their needs or their complementary skills or talents. To use Clothespin Grouping, list your grouping criteria on a chart or portable whiteboard. Then use clothespins with students' names on them, clipping the appropriate name to the selected criterion. Examples of grouping criteria could include

- Choice of topic or prompt
- Choice of question to address or choice of problem
- Assignment completion

Figure 5.10   Clothespin Board to Organize Student Groups or Centers

Food and customs	*Climate and vegetation*
History and origins	*Economics and geographic implications*
Influential leaders	*Crafts and artisans*

For a geography unit, for example, students might want to work within the categories shown in Figure 5.10. Their choices might be defined by the teacher or might be suggested as a result of student input and interest. Students would take their clothespin with their name on it and select the group with the topic that they would be most interested in studying. If the teacher chose to limit the size of each group, students could clip their clothespin to the area of the chart that indicates their choice or interest. They could then organize in small groups of three or four or perhaps choose to work alone for this investigation.

This grouping process can also be used to assign students to centers. They clip their clothespin to the center of choice for the next day, or the teacher assigns students to the center based on learning needs or appropriate sequence.

Students may also be grouped heterogeneously by using colored paper for assignment sheets. Students are given different colored assignment sheets based on ability level; for example,

- Students with higher ability in reading may be given yellow assignment sheets.
- Students with average ability may have blue sheets.
- Struggling readers may be given pink sheets.

Students would be asked to form a group of three that includes two other people who have a different colored paper. Teachers may also assign a different role with the cooperative task so that the groups foster interdependence.

SUMMARY

How, then, can teachers adjust the learning? Teachers can use the pre-assessment data they have collected for knowledge of their students' learning styles and multiple intelligences (see Chapter 2), and they can use the repertoire of grouping strategies that we presented in this chapter. These data can be used to make organizational and instructional decisions. In Chapter 6, we will examine instructional practices that show great promise in promoting student achievement. In Chapter 7, we will show you how to put it all together to plan lessons that give all students a better chance to achieve targeted standards.

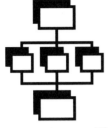

Instructional Strategies That Increase Student Learning

6

THE ART AND SCIENCE OF TEACHING

When we consider the process of learning, we realize that teaching has focused more on delivery to the masses than processing and understanding of new information and skills. Only through personal interaction and meaning does information become knowledge and have a lasting effect on the learner and in the long-term memory. In classrooms, we sometimes go for coverage rather than deep understanding. With our limited time, we go for coverage assuming that all learners are at the same starting point and have the same interests and background, and that they're able to comprehend and process at the same speed.

Teachers may be very knowledgeable about goals, objectives, and outcomes related to standards. Stigler and Hiebert (1999) report that although it is essential that teachers know the standards, it is equally important that the teaching/learning process provide learning opportunities to help all students reach the standards. Standards are the target, assessments help us "feed forward" toward the standards, but it is the quality and variety of teaching methods that allow teachers to help all students succeed. Teachers may have a repertoire of instructional strategies that they can use to present and provide students with processing time. This is the *science* of teaching. What teachers may be lacking, however, is the knowledge that would suggest

- Which instructional process would work best
- With what content
- With which students
- Under what circumstances

That is the *art* of teaching.

The challenge is to take the best practices in their best form and use them strategically to create learning for the diversity of classrooms in schools today. Students give us clues continually to help us understand how they might learn better and what would appeal to them and engage their attention. We will examine ways to collect data on student preferences and also strategies that hold the best-practice label and should be in a teacher's repertoire so that most students do succeed.

We also know that effective teachers have expertise that includes competencies in the following areas:

- *Instructional strategies.* Researchers—among them Bennett (1986), Creemers (1994), and Hattie (1992)—have outlined instructional strategies that are used in effective teaching and learning. Marzano et al. (2001) have assimilated these into nine categories. It is also important that teachers use a variety of instructional strategies during the various phases of the lesson.

- *Classroom management.* In many research studies, this attribute of effective teaching is rated most important (Wang, Haertel, & Walberg, 1993), as without it, the classroom is chaotic and little learning results. Classroom management includes distributing resources, controlling the movement of students, establishing discipline guidelines, creating groups, promoting attendance—all actions that help set the tone and climate of the classroom so that we better ensure all students can learn (Brophy, 1996; Doyle, 1986; Duke, 1979).

- *Classroom curriculum design.* Curriculum is often referred to as the plan for conveying content through the teacher-designed learning experiences that students are involved in at school (Caswell & Campbell, 1935; Olivia, 1982; Saylor & Alexander, 1974). Marzano (2003) defines curriculum as "decisions regarding sequencing, pacing, and experiences that are the purview of the classroom teacher" (p. 106).

MEMORY PROCESSES AND THE COGNITIVE LEARNING SYSTEM

Let's focus on how students learn and how teachers teach. The effective teacher focuses on memory, consciousness, and language development and uses stimulation of all senses to facilitate learning. Students cannot engage completely and at a high level unless all systems are involved in the learning process. Through the selection of appropriate strategies for learning and teaching, the activation of these processes is not left to chance.

Sensory Memory

We know that the brain pays attention to that which captures our attention. Data enters the sensory memory through the senses, which constantly scan the environment for potentially interesting or threatening stimuli. The sensory memory captures only that which is engaging through contact with the senses, emotions, or perceived meaning and relevance. Because the senses are constantly being bombarded with stimuli, few are given full attention. Only that which appeals to the learner—for whatever reason— will capture attention. Thus lessons and classes should begin in ways that are interesting and motivating so that the senses are stimulated. These beginnings serve to capture students' attention. Emotions are also helpful in garnering student attention and can be used in the opening of lessons and units of study for motivation and engagement. Any activity that stirs emotions or creates a meaningful context will often engage the learner and capture attention that otherwise would be lost.

Using focus activities to begin a class productively may help students "focus in" on the day's learning. These activities may include a quick

Figure 6.1   The Memory Processing System

Sensory Memory	Short-Term/Working Memory	Long-Term Memory
(To Garner Attention)	*(Rehearsal and Elaboration)*	*(Long-Term Retention)*
Novelty Relevance Meaning	Instructional processes that engage and process information to produce knowledge	Strategies to access and retrieve information from long-term memory
Challenge Problem Dilemma Story Question Puzzle Object Novelty Goals and expectations Advance organizers	Compare and contrast Concept attainment Concept formation Synectics Note taking Projects Multiple intelligences Advanced organizers Cooperative learning Visual representations Checkmate	Quick write KWL Journal Tickets out 3–2–1 Four corners Advance organizers

assessment tool, a reconnection with the previous day's lesson, or one of techniques listed in the Sensory Memory column of Figure 6.1. Examples include

- *Challenge.* Giving students a challenge that pertains to the topic helps to open their mental files so they can access what they already know or think they know about the topic.

- *Problem.* Asking students to solve a problem in pairs or small groups will help them focus their attention as well as give the teacher some pre-assessment data.

- *Dilemma.* Posing a situation for students to consider can help focus attention. For example, students might be asked to *think* to themselves and *share* with a partner about the question, "Can war be creative as well as destructive?"

- *Story.* Often, a story will set a context and engage the attention of students related to the topic. In a unit about freedom fighters of the American Revolution, the teacher read a story about Paul Revere to introduce and motivate students.

- *Question.* Posing an intriguing question can also capture attention and set a context for the lesson to come. For example, the teacher could ask students to predict what would happen if . . .

- *Puzzle.* A puzzle that is a way of introduction or review can be presented at the beginning of a class. For example, in a language arts class, students could be asked to work alone or in pairs to punctuate this passage: "that that is is that that is not is not is not that it"

- *Object.* At the beginning of a new topic, interesting objects or artifacts may be presented to engage the learner. For example, in a study of pioneer days, the teacher gathered a collection of objects from pioneer days: candle molds, apple peeler, anvil, iron griddle, butter churn, butter press, coal oil lamps, pioneer clothing. She had students examine the items and see if they could suggest their usefulness to pioneers.

- *Novelty.* Students respond well to novelty and situations and materials that are out of the ordinary. A teacher sporting a *Cat in the Hat* chapeau garners attention and creates a humorous moment. Costumes and novel activities create a unique experience and a memorable interlude.

- *Goals and expectations.* Stating the goals and expectations and posting the standards add relevance and meaning to the learning activities.

- *Advance organizers.* Advance organizers (Ausubel, 1960) invite students to see what they are expected to know and be able to do in the unit of study. It provides what Ausubel calls *meaningful reception learning*. There are three steps in the process. The first is to share the standards and objectives. The second is to present the organizer. A graphic organizer (word web or mind map) or an agenda map may be helpful in conveying a gestalt so that students get the big picture and understand how the learning will unfold. The third is to develop an awareness of the content of the unit of study. It may be a reading that students do in advance to give them some background information or a video that they watch to give them an overview.

Short-Term or Working Memory

If sensory memory grabs something interesting, meaningful, or engaging, that item moves into short-term or working memory. Then the learner is conscious of the data, but the consciousness will last for only seconds unless it is rehearsed and elaborated. This is an opportunity for learners to interact with the content or use skills to deepen their understanding and make meaning. This is where we provide drill and practice to develop skills or situations to elaborate further on new content and knowledge. Memorization usually has a short shelf life compared to the production of long-term memory through elaboration in meaningful ways. Multiple intelligences and student choice can be crucial in engaging students in a variety of ways.

Rehearsal is something that is often left out of classroom practice as time is limited and often we tend to "teach, test, and hope for the best." Yet we know from research that it takes many trials and practice sessions to reach mastery. In fact, if students only interact with the content one time, the increase in learning is only about 22%. To increase learning by 80% takes about twenty-four practice sessions (Marzano et al., 2001). Thus rehearsal and practice are needed, often using a variety of methods so that learning is retrieved often from long-term memory. This revisiting of concepts and information helps strengthen neural networks and makes information easier to retrieve over time. Some techniques for rehearsal and elaboration are listed in the middle column of Figure 6.1.

Long-Term Memory

Long-term memory includes both declarative and procedural memory. Declarative memory is the "who, what, when, and where" facts that we learn related to content and concepts. Procedural memory is the step-by-step process of executing a skill. The steps in the process are declarative when we are learning them but become automatic once we have practiced enough to make the procedure unconscious, such as the steps in long division. Once new learning has been rehearsed sufficiently and has gone into long-term memory, it remains unconscious until it is recalled again for application, problem solving, or use in a new situation. We can help to retrieve information from long-term memory through the techniques in the right-hand column of Figure 6.1. Examples include the following:

Figure 6.2 GEL Chart as a Variation on KWL

What have you Got?	What do you Expect?	What have you Learned?

- *Quick write.* A quick write is just as it says. Students take a minute or two to write what they are thinking. They may also write from a teacher prompt, such as, Do you agree with the author? Why or why not? What do you think will happen next? Describe in your own words what the author was trying to say.

- *KWL.* The KWL chart (Ogle, 1986) has three columns: K (What do you *Know*—or think you know?), W (What do you *Want* to know?) and L (What have you *Learned*?) We know a teacher named Gene from Virginia, who discovered that his high school students didn't *Know* nothin' and didn't *Want* to know nothin,' so he decided to use a GEL chart because he wanted things to GEL for his students (see Figure 6.2). Gene asked his students these questions: What have you *Got*?; What do you *Expect*?; and What have you *Learned*? That way he got the information he needed as pre-assessment, focus, and recall without having the "cool" students appear to be too zealous.

- *Journal.* Students can be asked to jot down in their journal what they remember or know about a topic or process that is part of the curriculum.

- *Tickets out.* Sometimes at the end of the day, students can jot down what they have learned and what they have enjoyed that day or what they are still curious about. This gives teachers data about the "temperature" and the learning. Use self-sticking notes so students can leave them on the bulletin board on the way out the door.

- *3–2–1.* This is a variation on the Ticket Out technique that teachers use to get feedback at the end of the day or to open mental files at the beginning of a class. It can also be a great way to pre-assess. Sample stems for 3–2–1 could include

  o 3 things you learned today
  o 2 connections that you made
  o 1 question that still puzzles you

   o 3 things you remember from last class
   o 2 connections you made
   o 1 question that is still puzzling you

   o 3 things you know about _____
   o 2 things you'd be interested in about _____
   o 1 person you'd like to work with on this project

 • *Knowledge preserver.* Like a life preserver, this is a visual organizer that students can use to organize information so that they can hold on to it. It allows them to focus on a topic and bring to conscious memory aspects that are important for them to know and organize.

 • *Advance organizers.* Advance organizers provide ways to see the big picture and to call up previous knowledge about a topic. They can take many forms, including agenda maps, graphic organizers, charts and notes, or diagrams and schema. At the beginning of a unit on the Second World War, for example, the teacher gave the students a "fish bone" organizer that showed them the different elements they would be studying in the unit (see Figure 6.3). As they progressed through the unit, students filled in the fish bone as an ongoing record of their learning. The advance organizer is a key piece for note taking and summarizing and for review and study purposes. It could also be used in the study of a novel to build character studies. Or it could be used for problem solving, with the problem stated in the fish head and the alternatives displayed on each bone.

Figure 6.3 "Fish Bone" Advance Organizer for a Unit on the Second World War

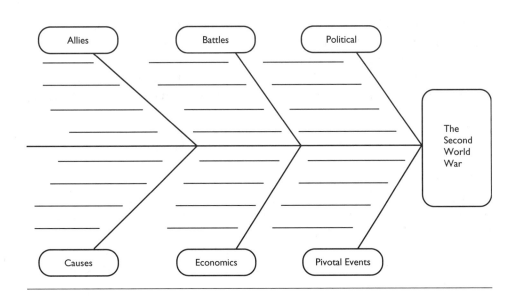

DIFFERENTIATING INSTRUCTIONAL STRATEGIES

Strategies That Stimulate Student Interest

Using a variety of instructional strategies stimulates student interest from one unit to the next. Students' interests are related to the investments they make in their work at school as well as to the teacher's repertoire of instructional strategies to entice and engage learners (Wasley, Hampel, & Clark, 1997). If students come into the classroom and are asked to do the same thing day after day, the novelty wears off, and complacency and boredom move in. If they are always listening to the teacher or reading and answering questions from the textbook, students are not necessarily actively engaged, either physically or mentally, and there is little dendritic growth.

Many research studies show that lecture and reading produce relatively low percentages of retention. According to the National Training Labs in Bethel, Maine, retention rates are as follows:

5% lecture

10% reading

20% audiovisual

30% demonstration

50% discussion

75% practice by doing

90% teaching others

Thus "Sit and Get" does not seem to be the most effective way to receive, learn, and retain new information. If it were so, we would see all students having success with this approach.

We have no research to support a teacher-centered distribution. Only the successes of students who learn in spite of us, who are concrete-sequential enough to play the school game, support this approach. Sufficient rehearsal and practice time are missing for many students, and that is the time needed to move information to knowledge and deep understanding in long-term memory. Time is also necessary to develop skills to the automatic level. "Spray and Pray" does not necessarily move the student through the levels of thinking outlined by Bloom (1985). When teachers stand and deliver, students generally only attend to the recall level of thinking, if that. With this approach, the opportunity to discuss, practice, and teach others is missing, and students won't necessarily have the meaning and understanding that will hook the information in long-term memory.

Strategies That Increase Student Learning

In *Classroom Instruction That Works* (Marzano et al., 2001), the authors detail nine instructional strategies that can be used effectively to increase student learning. Their book covers both the research and a wide range of examples in a variety of subject areas. These strategies can have a profound impact on student learning, as the percentile gains in student achievement detailed below demonstrate (Marzano et al., 2001):

1. *Recognizing similarities and differences, using metaphors and analogies* (45 percentile gains). This strategy allows students to examine information for similarities and differences among any number of ideas or things. This process allows students opportunities for deep processing of information and helps them connect new learning with things that were learned previously.

2. *Summarizing and note taking* (37 percentile gains). This strategy is extremely useful to help students identify key concepts and information that is relevant and important for them to record and remember. Many students have little skill in this area, and teachers sometimes assume that students have figured out a strategy on their own. However, many students (especially Beach Balls) are random thinkers and do not have strategies to organize information to increase retention.

3. *Reinforcing effort and providing recognition* (29 percentile gains). Students often attribute success or failure to luck or ability whereas research shows that effort is the key ingredient in success. Everyone needs feedback and recognition for their efforts, and teachers who give specific targeted feedback help students continue to persevere and succeed. Students also need to develop skills of metacognition so that they can analyze their own efforts and progress and continue to set goals.

4. *Homework and practice* (28 percentile gains). Providing homework and practice is essential to help students gain the rehearsal they need to transfer information into long-term memory. In classrooms, there is never enough time for this process of twenty-four rehearsals. However, homework should not just be more of the same work done in class or work that was not completed. It also may be differentiated depending on what different students need.

5. *Nonlinguistic representations* (27 percentile gains). This strategy taps into both hemispheres of the brain. Adding pictures, diagrams, and organizers to written work can be useful for visual/spatial and logical/mathematical learners, adding a rich dimension to note taking and information organizing.

6. *Cooperative learning* (27 percentile gains). This strategy of facilitating interactive learning of heterogeneous small groups has been well documented for twenty-five years in helping students learn and develop the social skills necessary to be successful in the real world.

7. *Setting objectives and providing feedback* (23 percentile gains). Students can usually hit any target that is clear and holds still long enough (Stiggins, 1993). Providing objectives and ongoing feedback helps students "feed forward" toward the goal.

8. *Generating and testing hypotheses* (23 percentile gains). Intriguing students by asking them to develop hunches based on information and then to test their theories is a great way to engage learners and have them take ownership for their learning.

9. *Questions, cues, and advance organizers* (22 percentile gains). These techniques help students to open mental files and help teachers to pre-assess knowledge and skills that students already possess or lack. It gives students the big picture and perhaps a road map for the learning journey.

RECOGNIZING SIMILARITIES AND DIFFERENCES/USING METAPHORS AND ANALOGIES

The ability to recognize and identify the similarities and differences between different things is the thinking skill of comparing and contrasting. This is how we learn and are able to define concepts. Venn diagrams, flow and cross-classification charts, concept attainment and concept formation, metaphors, and analogies are all ways that can be used to express similarities and differences.

Visual and graphic representations can also be helpful in depicting and facilitating this process. Visual and graphic organizers are logical mathematical tools that appeal to many learners as a way of organizing information. Recent research indicates that when graphic organizers are used (including electronic forms), students show increases in retention and comprehension, and they demonstrate higher levels of achievement on content-based assessments (Stiggins, 1993).

Comparing and Contrasting

Comparing and contrasting is a thinking skill that is a key to increasing student achievement (Marzano et al., 2001). Several graphic organizers facilitate that thinking. Ultimately, teachers want students to select the appropriate organizer that will work for them. Some learners may need more structure than others.

The "Comparing and Contrasting Two Things" graphic organizer shown in Figure 6.4 supports students who may need more scaffolding:

Figure 6.4 Comparing and Contrasting Two Things

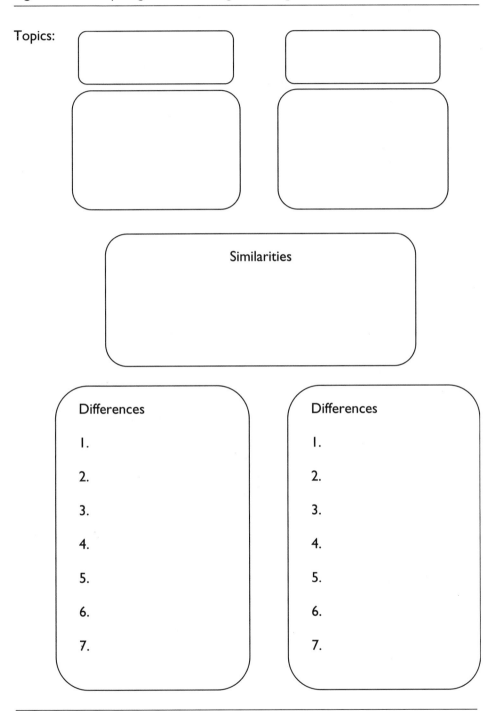

SOURCE: Reprinted from *Differentiated Instruction Strategies: One Size Doesn't Fit All*, by Gayle H. Gregory and Carolyn Chapman.

1. First, students place the two things to be compared in the top two boxes marked "Topics."

2. Then they use the *BOW* so that they can take a BOW for success.

3. They (B) *Brainstorm* in the boxes below the topic box to list everything they know about the topics.

4. Then they (O) *Organize* the information by selecting the similarities and placing them in the common center box.

5. Then they organize the differences in the bottom boxes, aligning the contrasting items.

6. From there, they are able to (W) *Write* a comparison essay or prepare a presentation.

Other students may prefer a Venn diagram to show their thinking (Figure 6.5), but they may also need some key areas defined for their scrutiny. For example, students might be asked to compare and contrast two explorers with regard to the following aspects: country of origin, sponsor, quest, route, dates, and accomplishments. For some situations, a cross-classification chart may be preferable (Figure 6.6). In this chart, several things can be compared for certain criteria, and then similarities and differences can be noted. For example, students may take four food groups, such as meats and poultry, milk products, grain products, and fruits and vegetables, and place them in the boxes down the left-hand side. Across the top, the categories will be sources, functions, nutrients, and deficiency diseases. A cross-classification chart can also be used as a note taking and summarizing piece or as a review.

Inductive Thinking

Inductive thinking is a process that allows students to make sense of information by organizing it into groupings (words, concrete items, ideas, and so on) that have similar attributes or characteristics. We tend to do this with most things in our life, from our kitchen and workshop to our bookshelves, closets, or desks. Larger organizations, such as grocery, department, video, and hardware stores, also group things. Of course, Clipboards are more amenable to this than are Beach Balls, and they may come up with quite different categories into which they ultimately organize things.

Concept Attainment

One strategy that teachers have used for many years is concept attainment, which was first introduced in 1966 by Jerome Bruner. It is a method

Figure 6.5 Venn Diagram for Comparing and Contrasting

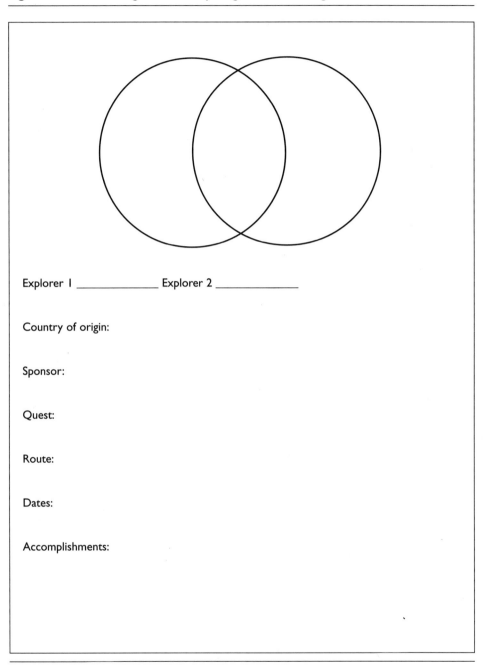

Explorer 1 _____ Explorer 2 _____

Country of origin:

Sponsor:

Quest:

Route:

Dates:

Accomplishments:

Figure 6.6 Cross-Classification Chart for Comparing and Contrasting

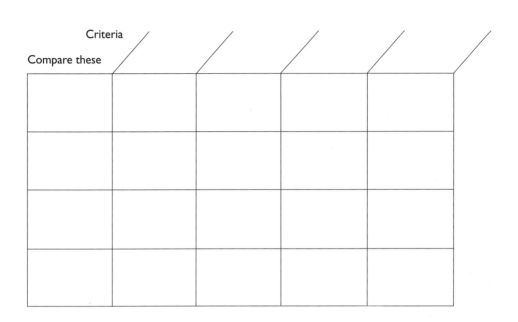

of identifying critical attributes of a concept and then forming generalizations. We learn the difference between concepts by mentally recording their similarities and differences. Thus we identify schnauzers, poodles, and greyhounds as dogs because we are able to identify their similarities and the critical attributes that they all have in common. Concept attainment facilitates the development of inductive thinking by providing critical attributes that enable us to form concepts and to understand why an item is part of the general category or concept. This strategy is teacher controlled and facilitated whereas concept formation is more student controlled. The teacher presents examples and nonexamples, or "yes" and "no" examples, until students can identify the critical attributes of the yes examples.

This strategy can be used to introduce a concept, to check for understanding, or to review material. There are three phases or steps in the concept attainment process:

1. *Present the data.* In this phase, the teacher decides on the yes and no examples that will be used in the process (see Figure 6.7). Also, teachers need to decide what order to present the data in and what medium to use: overhead, whiteboard, real objects, slides, poster, role-play, or video. Often a focus question, clue, or statement may be given to help students to narrow the field as they try to identify the concept; for example, the clue or focus statement for the sample in Figure 6.7 could be "This has nothing to do with numbers."

Figure 6.7 Sample Data for Concept Attainment

Yes Examples	No Examples
2	3
4	5
8	9
week	month
fair	ground
hare	hat
there	dish
hear	every
pair	apple
golf	swim
page	letter

2. *Share and confirm the hypotheses.* After each yes and no example has been given, the teacher may ask the students if they have an idea about what the concept might be. This can be tested without necessarily depriving the other students of the quest. For example, the teacher can ask students to

- "Thumbs up" if you think you have an idea.
- Give a yes example that would fit the concept.
- Write your answer down on a draw/erase board and hold it up.
- Share your idea with a partner and see what your partner thinks about it.

The teacher has to judge the best order in which to present the examples, always having an additional example ready to further extend students' thinking.

3. *Apply and extend.* After the students identified the concept of "words that sound the same but have different spellings and meanings," the teacher would introduce the new vocabulary, *homonyms.* The students could then work in pairs to see how many they could generate and use in sentences to show their, there, meaning.

The concept attainment strategy is novel and often appeals to the students' curiosity and the brain's need to find patterns and solve problems. Also, the students tend to recall the concept and understand it more deeply because of the inductive process used to learn it. This strategy can be used in science, math, social studies, or any subject or discipline to develop understanding of new or previously learned concepts; for example,

- *Language arts.* Expository statements, transition words, adjectives, metaphors, and similes
- *Science.* Magnetic items, biodegradable items, mammals, or bonding
- *Social studies.* Justice, democracy, explorers, or equality
- *Psychology.* Honor or privilege
- *Music.* Jazz composers
- *Math.* Prime numbers

Note that concrete examples such as cars are a better place to start than abstract concepts such as love. Use Figure 6.8 to plan concept attainment.

Concept Formation

Another inductive thinking strategy is concept formation, introduced by Hilda Taba (1967). It is also a classification process where items are grouped based on student thinking about like attributes. Concept formation is more student focused than concept attainment, as students have more control over the data. It is also a powerful strategy that allows students to discuss, share, question, and analyze their ideas as they move toward forming a new concept.

The usual steps in the process are the following:

Phase 1: Present the data. Offer a focus statement. Invite students to organize the data and name the groups.

Phase 2: Develop a hypothesis and share their thinking.

Phase 3: Apply the concept and promote discussion. Some teachers prefer to use the acronym GROUP to set up the process:

(G) Gather data (given, brainstormed, discovered, collected)

(R) Reexamine

(O) Organize by similarities

(U) Use a label to name the group

(P) Process, discuss, and apply

A sample activity to show the students how the process works might be to ask them to organize themselves into groups based on reasons that they can identify. There is no one way to do this, but students need to be able to explain and rationalize their thinking. For example, students could be grouped by

- Gender
- Hair color

Figure 6.8   Thinking and Planning for Concept Attainment

1. What is the purpose of this activity?

   Where in the unit or lesson will I use it?

   What concept do I want students to know and understand?

2. Create a data set of yes and no examples (words, pictures, objects) and decide the order in which they should be presented

3. What means will you use to present the data?

4. Decide on statements or questions to test students' hypotheses

5. How will students apply their understanding of the concept?

- Height
- Nationality
- Birth month

They would then work through the process as follows:

Phase 1: Present the Data

In this phase, students are given the data. They can obtain it in different ways:

- From the teacher, for example, words on whiteboard, overhead, chart paper, or actual objects
- From the text, for example, students read and list the data
- By collecting it as they watch a video alone or in pairs
- By collecting it on a field trip or walk; for example, items from the woods
- By generating it in a brainstorming activity in pairs, or small groups, or as a total group

Phase 2: Invite Students to Organize the Data and Name the Groups

Explain to students that there is no right or wrong way to organize the material. What is important is the thinking that goes on as students make decisions about the groupings. They are cautioned about labeling at the beginning until the final organization is complete. Students need to constantly review why they are grouping the way they are. What is their rationale, and what are the attributes that caused them to be in a particular group? What are the relationships that exist? What inferences are made?

Phase 3: Invite Students to Apply the Concepts Garnered From the Groups

Students are encouraged to explain and rationalize their organization and the concepts that they have formed. They should also verify their thinking and suggest other things that would fit into their organization. Examples of concept formation may include

- Coins
- Short paragraphs
- Foods
- Rocks
- Types of equations
- Words

Synectics

William Gordon (1961) developed a process he called synectics, which helps develop creativity through the use of metaphors and analogies. It helps to deepen understanding of a new or abstract concept by relating it to a well-known item or idea. This is a powerful memory hook, as an analogy is a mental file that, when opened, holds a great deal of information concerning the attributes of an idea or item. In Chapter 2, for example, we used the analogies of a Beach Ball, Microscope, Clipboard, and Puppy to help you retain the characteristics of different learning styles.

Teachers can help students understand processes and concepts by linking them to something that students know well. For example, one teacher wanted students to understand not only the process of problem solving but also the feelings involved in persisting through the problem-solving process. Students built analogies together in small groups as a pre-assessment activity.

One group used the connection "Problem solving is like untying a knot because . . .":

- At first it looks like a mess.
- You have to figure out where to begin.
- You must decide the step-by-step process.
- Order matters; you have to look ahead.
- You have to be careful not to make it more complicated.
- You have to have patience and not get discouraged.

Another group said, "Problem solving is like a treasure hunt because . . .":

- You have to look at options from clues you have.
- You need to make a plan.
- You have to be willing to risk failure.
- Sometimes it is trial and error.
- Sometimes you have to start all over again.
- Sometimes you get the gold!

SUMMARIZING AND NOTE TAKING

Marzano et al. (2001) point out that all students need strategies to capture relevant information and record it for future reference. Many students have difficulty selecting the important information and organizing it in a way that can be recalled or accessed. Different forms of note taking may be provided for students so that they can experience a variety of ways of organizing information and be selective in terms of what works best for them. That way, they will have a resource bank of strategies for future use.

W5 Organizer

Using a W5 model (who, what, where, when, why) is suitable for note taking about some types of content. A matrix may be provided as an advance organizer (see Figure 6.9) for students to collect information in an organized fashion. Figure 6.10 shows how students could use a W5 organizer in a social studies lesson on the Cuban missile crisis to compare the Cuban, American, and Russian involvement.

Split-Page Organizer

Students may also use a split-page note taker (see Figure 6.11) to jot down key words and to use visual representations to illustrate their understanding of information. When students are listening to a lecture, viewing a video, or reading a text, teachers can help them summarize and take notes accurately by providing a boxed split-page organizer with headings to capture information (see Figure 6.12). Figure 6.13 shows how a boxed organizer can be used for key words or drawings for a social studies unit about the Second World War.

Four-Corners Organizer

Gregory and Chapman (2002) introduced a four-corners organizer (see Figure 6.14) that can be used for note taking and summarizing about a character sketch when students are reading a story or novel. The four-corners organizer can be used in any subject discipline to organize and record information. See Figures 6.15 through 6.18 for examples from math, health, science, and social studies.

HOMEWORK AND PRACTICE

To be effective, according to Cawelti (1995), homework should be

- Modeled and explained clearly in class
- Explicit, with well-defined objectives for all students
- Sure to create "perfect practice" using material that is familiar to the students
- Facilitated and supported (not completed) by parents in terms of time and place for completion
- Connected to the day's learning but not just more of the same

Figure 6.9 W5 Organizer for Note Taking and Summarizing

Topic:			
Who:			
What?			
Where?			
When?			
Why?			
Summary:			

Figure 6.10   W5 Organizer for Sample Unit on the Cuban Missile Crisis

Topic	Cuban Missile Crisis		
Who:	United States	Cuba	Russia
What?			
Where?			
When?			
Why?			
Summary:			

Figure 6.11 Split-Page Organizer for Key Words and Graphics

Jot Down Key Words	Use a Graphic Organizer

- Adjusted to the level that will engage and challenge students
- Responded to with feedback to help students deepen their understanding and competency

Marzano et al. (2001) also offer several approaches to homework:

- A homework policy should be established and communicated.
- The purpose should be clear.
- Homework assignment sheets should be used.
- Feedback on homework should be consistent.

NONLINGUISTIC REPRESENTATIONS

Nonlinguistic representations take many forms. They include charts, drawings, diagrams, graphic organizers, and pictorial representations that

(Text continues on page 163)

Figure 6.12   Boxing the Lecture Split-Page Organizer

Figure 6.13   Boxing the Lecture Organizer for Sample Unit on the Second World War

Allies	Causes
Battles	Pivotal Events
Advances	Results

Figure 6.14 Four-Corners Organizer for Character Sketch

Character Sketch

Character: _____

1 Conclusions		Evidence	**2**
Evidence			Conclusions
	Looks like	Does	
Evidence	Seems like	Sounds like	Conclusions
	Conclusions	Evidence	
3			**4**

Figure 6.15 Four-Corners Organizer for Sample Math Unit

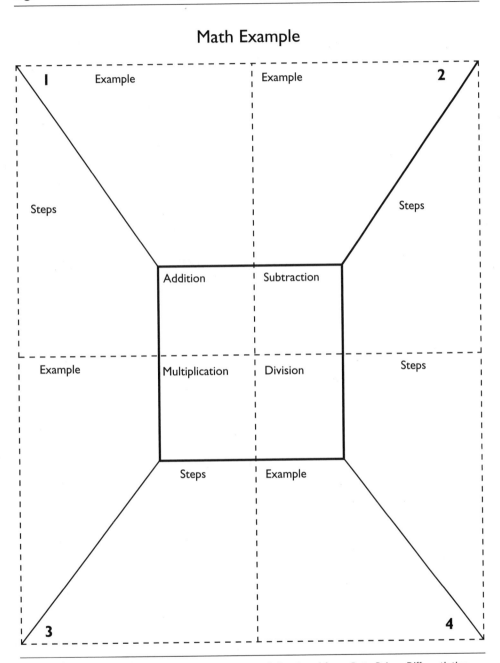

Math Example

Figure 6.16 Four-Corners Organizer for Sample Health Unit on Nutrition

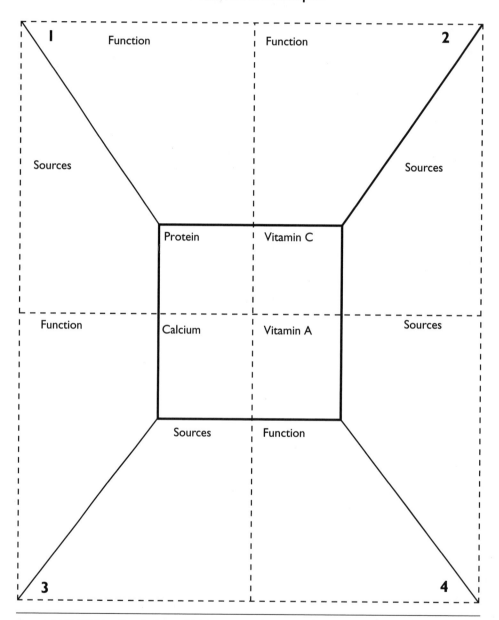

Nutrition Example

Figure 6.17 Four-Corners Organizer for Sample Science Unit on Physics Laws

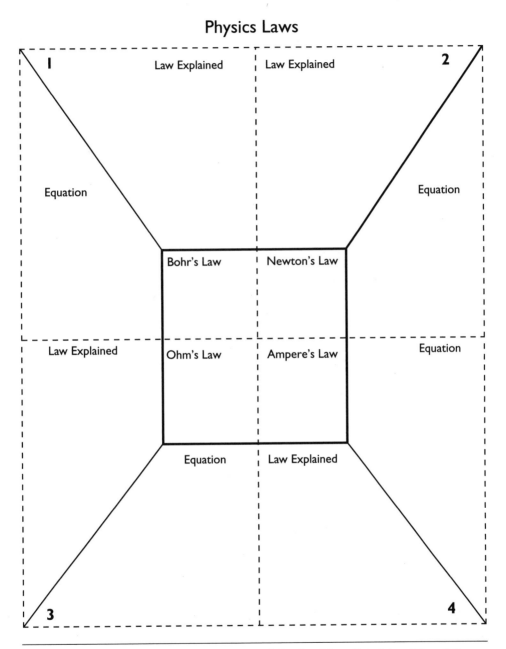

Physics Laws

Figure 6.18 Four-Corners Organizer for Sample Social Studies Unit on Explorers

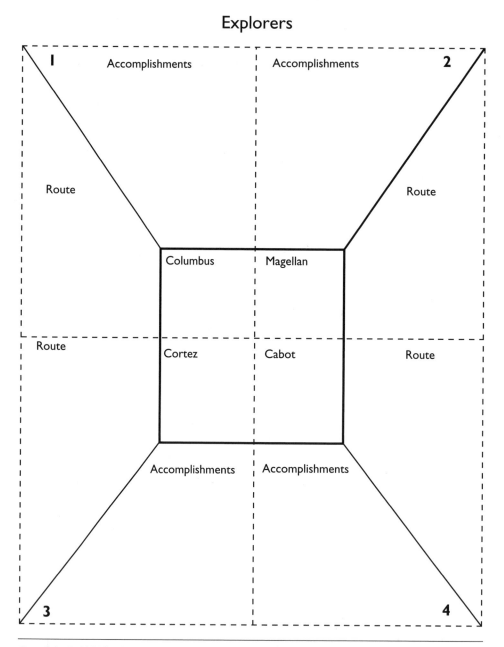

Figure 6.19 Sunshine Wheel

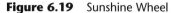

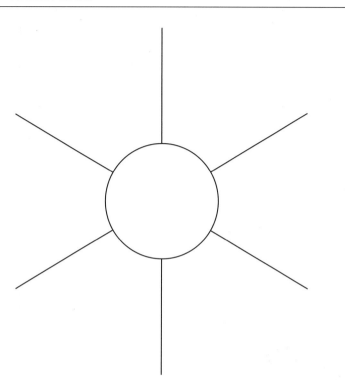

help students organize data. They are metacognitive tools that show student thinking in visual form. Visual representations can be used to process information, to review information, to summarize information, to take notes, or to use as reflective tools. They can even be used as advance organizers, pre-assessment tools, and student notes.

Sunshine Wheel

The sunshine wheel (see Figure 6.19) is often used for brainstorming the attributes of a concept or idea. Students can use the sunshine wheel in any subject area by placing the concept in the center bubble and recording an attribute on each one of the rays.

Impact Wheel

Like the sunshine wheel, the impact wheel begins with a bubble in the middle that gives a statement or situation that exists or a prediction of what might happen. The central bubble has several categories where the implications may be evident (see Figure 6.20). Around each secondary bubble, supporting information is generated. For example, the center

Figure 6.20 Impact Wheel

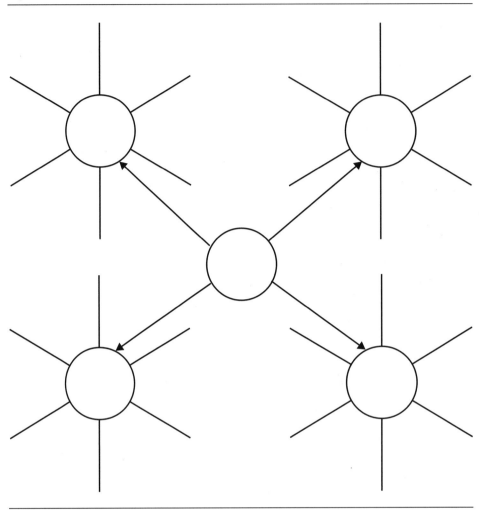

bubble may record "Berlin Wall Falls" (Figure 6.21). In each of the secondary bubbles, students could place supporting information from the economic, political, societal, and foreign policy spheres.

The impact wheel can also be used for problem solving or decision making by putting the problem or dilemma in the middle and then the options or alternatives, one in each bubble, supporting each alternative with information attached to each bubble. Another use of the impact wheel may be to organize information for writing. Students can place the title of the story in the center bubble and then the main characters, one in each bubble, and then their attributes on the rays of each bubble. Or in science, it may be used to record the areas of study for reptiles. The center bubble would have the reptiles in it, and then the secondary bubbles would have the following: habitat, food, reproduction, and characteristics.

Figure 6.21 Impact Wheel for Sample Concept "Berlin Wall Falls"

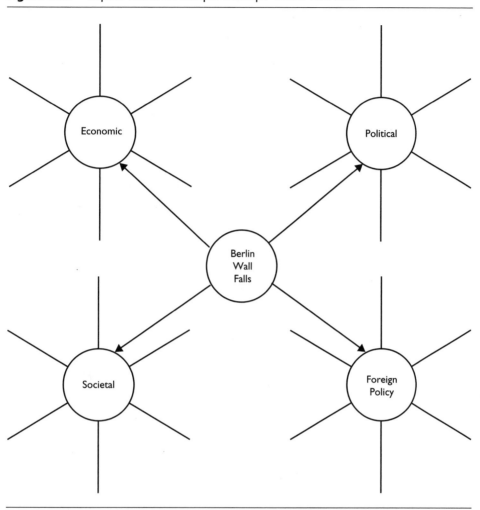

Mind Maps

Mind mapping was first introduced by Tony Buzan (1974) as a way of using both sides of the brain to process information and organize ideas. In transferring the information from the verbal to the pictorial, the brain relies on both hemispheres for processing the information. The brain likes to see both the big picture and also the component parts of concepts. The visuals, created with vivid color and unique drawings, can often be easily recalled in the mind's eye, and they bring back the information that the student needs to recall for future use.

Students can display connections, processes, and procedures as visual representations organized around a central concept. Or they can use color, line, connectors (such as links and chains), key words, and patterns to create visuals that represent a concept or process. Mind maps can be used in all subject areas for note taking and summarizing, for reviewing information, or for consolidation, for example,

- In social studies, to display the influence of Native Americans
- In science, to show the process of photosynthesis
- In math, to illustrate a problem-solving model
- In language arts, to show the story line of a novel
- In health, to show the components of a healthy diet
- In visual arts, to represent the attributes of a particular period

Using a mind map is usually a three-step process:

Step 1: Draw or depict in some way the concept or process identified.

Step 2: Brainstorm verbally the ideas or component parts that will make up the mind map.

Step 3: Draw visual representations of the ideas that will surround the central idea. The drawings may be randomly placed or placed in sequence to illustrate a process (see Figure 6.22).

Figure 6.22 Mind Map of Key Events in the Career of Abraham Lincoln

COOPERATIVE GROUP LEARNING

PIGSF (PIGS Face) is an acronym that stands for the five elements of cooperative group learning, according to the work of cooperative learning experts David and Roger Johnson (1991, 1998). Acronyms (a form of mnemonics) are helpful in memory recall, as they link or group information together with trigger clues so that recall is facilitated.

Five Elements of Cooperative Learning

P stands for positive interdependence. Students need one another to be successful in the task. We can help create positive interdependence by helping students to be clear about the goal of the activity. Teachers help students work together productively by giving them roles and tasks that facilitate the learning. Teachers might provide resources that have to be shared by the group and perhaps an incentive or simulation that could create a novel interest in the learning activity.

I stands for individual accountability. Students actively participate in the learning and take ownership for their part and ultimately the goal. Often, students loaf through a group activity because they aren't being held accountable at the end of the lesson. If someone else has already been named reporter, then the other students may consider themselves off the hook. If the reporter is not appointed at the beginning of the task, that means that anyone in the group may be asked to report, and all students must be attentive during the learning episode so that all can be ready to report.

This increases on-task behavior from all students in the group. Individual accountability also may be set up as an individual quiz after the group activity: The group activity is for learning, and the individual quiz is the assessment tool.

G stands for group processing. The cooperative group experience helps students discuss and reflect on the social skills that they have been practicing during the group activity. We know that we get better through practice, but we get even better if we reflect on that practice. Just taking a few minutes, the teacher can allow students to reflect about the following:

- How they used social skills
- How they could do better next time
- How they contributed to the group
- How they need this skill in their life

This could be done through group dialogue, personal reflection, and journaling.

S stands for social skills. Part of the trouble with group work is that it sometimes is not cooperative. Students don't necessarily have the social skills that they need to facilitate the learning process when they work with others. Even the skill of active listening is not commonplace with all our students, as they have spent many an hour in front of screens, whether television or computer. Active listening to others may not be something they have practiced; they may not even be conscious of it. Persistence is also a skill that students need to focus on learning and to complete complex tasks. As suggested in the section "Intelligent Behaviors" in Chapter 2, teachers may want to identify the indicators associated with each behavior (see Figure 2.17). Any of the social skills that students might need can be developed into a pie chart that provides specific indicators of the behavior.

F stands for face-to-face interaction. In cooperative groups students work "eye to eye" and "knee to knee" summarizing, discussing, problem solving, producing, and using critical thinking skills.

Simple Cooperative Structures

Simple strategies in cooperative learning don't require major setup or interaction and can be used at any time to stimulate dialogue, reflection, and interpersonal activity. Any of these may be kept handy to pull out and use quickly, as the situation warrants. They also satisfy the needs of the physical, social, and cognitive theaters with purposeful movement to facilitate learning.

Check Mate

Students work with a partner to answer a question or solve a problem or check homework. This strategy may also be used to practice and coach a new skill that has been taught. A two-to-four process can also be used to snowball or grow the group and teach or share the partner information. After partners work together, they meet with another partner set (two plus two) and teach and discuss their ideas with the new pair.

Round Robin or Table

In Round Robin (Kagan, 1994), each person in a small group takes a turn to answer a question or brainstorm an idea. Or each person does one step in a process in turn. For example, the students are to draw the setting for a story. Each student in turn would suggest one aspect of the setting and, with group approval, would draw it.

Tag Talk

Students work with a partner, and one person begins talking while the other actively listens. When the signal is given, students switch roles: The listener becomes the speaker, and the first speaker now listens. A variation could be to tag write. One person writes, and the other reads; then they switch roles.

Reciprocal Teaching

Students form groups of twos either randomly or constructed. Each student studies a particular piece of information and teaches the other the part that he or she studied. Together, they question one another and ensure that the concepts and ideas are clear and understood. This gives students a chance to rehearse and teach so that knowledge is constructed and can remain as long-term understanding.

Inside-Outside Circle

This simple tactic, which originated with Spencer Kagan (1994), is excellent for processing or reviewing information, generating ideas, or solving problems. It is accomplished by forming two circles with the same number of students in each (usually six or seven is a good number). One circle is formed inside the other, with students in one circle facing the students in the other. Inside-outside circles provide opportunities for dialogue, social interaction, and physical movement (see Figure 6.23).

Figure 6.23   Inside-Outside Circle

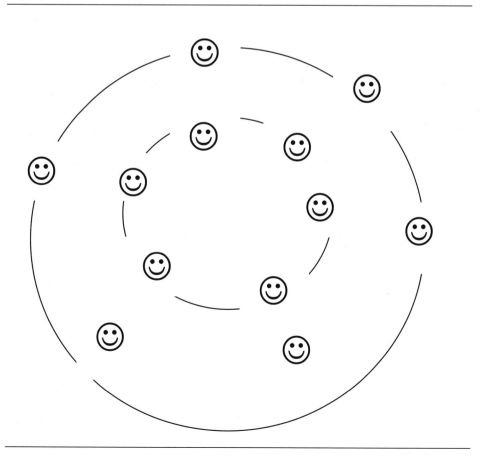

The students in the inside circle may be asked to share their response to a particular question with the students opposite them in the outside circle. Then students reverse roles. Another scenario might be that the each student needs ideas, suggestions, or a critique for their writing. Or as a review, students can create a question to ask their partners. It is a good idea to have the outside circle rotate so that everyone has a new partner, and the same question may be posed.

Jigsaw

Jigsaw (Aronson, 1978; Slavin, 1986) is a more complex strategy that can be used successfully with more advanced students who have developed the required social skills. It can be used to address large amounts of content in less time. It gives students an opportunity to delve into a piece of content at a greater level of expertise and truly understand it enough to help others, in turn, understand.

In Jigsaw, the teacher constructs groups of three or four (more than that cuts down on airtime and lessens the chances of students remaining on task). Ideally, these groups should be heterogeneous in formation so that students bring different learning styles and abilities to the group (see Figure 6.24). The process proceeds as follows:

Step 1: Base groups form.

Step 2: Students number off one to four.

Step 3: Students are assigned a task to go with their number.

Step 4: Students move to an expert group where they meet with others who have the same number.

Step 5: In their expert group, they read, discuss, research, or complete the assigned task.

Step 6: They return to their base groups and teach the other members what they have learned.

This strategy allows students to share the learning task and facilitates the interdependence necessary to make sure the group works well together.

Figure 6.24 Jigsaw Strategy for Cooperative Learning With Advanced Learners

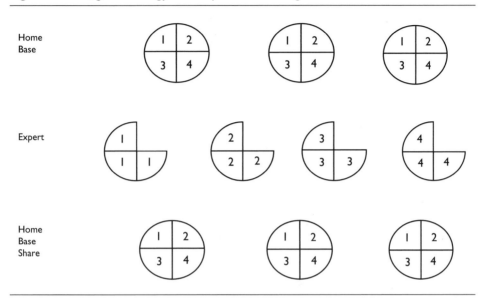

SUMMARY

Teachers recognize that there is no one right way to reach all students in one lesson. Teachers have a greater chance of optimizing student learning when they select from a huge array of instructional strategies that make a difference in student achievement. The art of teaching comes into play when we select and design the appropriate strategies related to the content and skills needed to help students reach targeted standards. The artful teacher paints with a palette of research-based instructional and learning strategies to enhance the success of his or her students, based on information that has been collected on individual learners, their interests and preferences, and their assessment data.

Data Driven Lesson Planning for Differentiated Learning 7

In the absence of conscious choices about how students need to learn and how we need to teach, all we have is a random selection of strategies we think might work. It is essential that we use data from a variety of sources to make real connections between where groups of students are now and where they will need to be for the final assessment of a standards-based unit.

While it takes some up-front work to approach teaching and learning in a data driven and standards-based manner, the payoff is high. As we adjust our units in terms of resources, timing, student communication, and evidence of learning, more students will demonstrate the academic growth necessary in this high-stakes political and social environment. As teachers, we need to be true diagnostic practitioners and thinkers to achieve the results we desire for every student. The level of decision making in classrooms where teachers make conscious choices about grouping, materials, and strategies is higher and more productive. This type of decision making will add clarity and precision to the art and science of planning and teaching.

USING DATA FOR LESSON PLANNING

As teachers build learning profiles of students, pre-assess, and develop a repertoire of instructional best practices, they are better able to meet the needs of the learners in their classrooms. Let's review each of the elements that we've covered in this book so far (see Figure 7.1).

- In Chapter 1, we used data to assess and build a supportive climate for student learning.
- In Chapter 2, we became more familiar with the student data on individual intelligences.
- In Chapter 3, we discussed a range of assessment tools that can help the learning "feed forward" and advance more rapidly.
- In Chapter 4, we designed sample curriculum units of study based on standards, allowing for ongoing data collection.
- In Chapter 5, we pre-assessed, developed adjustable learning grids, and explored flexible grouping strategies.
- In Chapter 6, we examined additional instructional best practices based on the data we have collected about our students.

Now we are ready to design differentiated learning experiences based on all this data and expertise.

Figure 7.2 is our template for planning differentiated learning. We can use it to plan strategically for our day-to-day instruction, not just for one class or one lesson but for a series of learning experiences so that students can continue to grow toward targeted standards. These chunks and lessons fall out of the unit plan as a logical progression for student learning. Thus the unit plan is the big picture, and the lesson plans are the natural grouping of knowledge and skill acquisition.

ESSENTIAL ELEMENTS FOR DATA DRIVEN LESSON PLANNING

Here are the elements that we think need to be addressed in the learning process.

Standards. In the lesson plan, the standard or benchmark may be narrower and more focused than the standards we outlined for unit planning in Chapter 4.

Assessment tools. These are the tools that we will use to collect data to provide continuous feedback to the student and to the teacher so that modifications to the lesson plan can be made based on that data.

Critical questions. These are the higher-level questions that we will develop up front and make visible to the students so that they are continually searching for meaning. Students can also be encouraged to create personal questions that are important to them and that define relevance and meaning for the unit of study.

Content. These are the facts, vocabulary, and essential skills of the unit.

Figure 7.1 Differentiating With Data for Student Growth and Achievement

Data to Create Climate	Data to Know the Learner	Assessment Data	Curriculum Design	Adjustable Assignments	Instructional Strategies
Building connections • Risk taking • Theaters of the mind • Resilience • Nurture Foster and sustain growth • Feedback • Reflective learning • Rituals • Respect • Cultural history • States of mind • Celebration • Higher level thinking	Learning styles • Strengths • Needs • Attitudes • Preferences Eight multiple intelligences Intelligent behavior • Persistence • Listening • Metacognition • Flexibility • Accuracy and precision • Posing questions and problems • Experience and new application • Sensory • Creativity • Efficacy	Diagnostic thinking • Pre-assessment • Formative assessment • Formal versus informal data collection • Performance assessments Analyze formative data • Grouping • Selecting differentiation strategies • Critical thinking The role of other forms of assessment • Using summative data • Self-assessment	Curriculum mapping • Standards-based • Focus and target • Expectations Unit planning • Standards • Benchmarks or objectives • Key concepts • Skills • Critical questions • The role of critical thinking • Relevance • Final assessment • Rubric • Pre-assessment • Chunking a unit • Transition points	TAPS • Total group • Alone • Pairs • Small group Adjustable grids • Compacting • Adjusting for competency • Content and materials • Communication and technology • Multiple intelligences • Readiness • Interest and choice • Process and rehearsal	Best practices strategies for • Sensory memory • Short-term memory • Long-term memory Research-based strategies • Inductive thinking • Note taking and summarizing • Homework • Nonlinguistic representations • Cooperative group learning Unit lesson planning

Figure 7.2   Template for Planning Differentiated Learning

Planning for Differentiated Learning	
Unit Title:	**Grade Level:**
Standards: What should students know and be able to do for this portion of the unit (chunk)?	**Pre-Assessment Lesson Strategy:** Use the data from the adjustable grid designed from the unit pre-assessment tool to start the unit and data from formative assessments throughout the unit such as journals, ticket out, quick writes, quizzes
Critical Question for This Portion of the Unit:	**Personal Question(s):**
Content: (Concepts)	**Skills:** (What will students do?)
Activate: (Creating focus and purpose)	
Acquire: (Getting the information and grouping choices)	
Formative Assessment: (Demonstrating the learning)	

Activating student interest/creating focus and purpose. Teachers need to pre-assess so that they know what students know, can do, or are interested in learning. This may be done well enough ahead of the unit of study so that the data can be used to plan the lessons that students need. This information can be used to consider grouping options, to decide on what learning experiences different students need, and to select activities that will create interest and attention for the unit that is coming up. In Carol Tomlinson's (2002) words, "Engagement happens when a lesson captures students' imaginations, snares their curiosity, ignites their opinions, and taps into their souls. Engagement is the magnet that attracts learners' meander- ing attention and holds it so that enduring learning can occur" (p. 38). Students can become engaged and excited about their learning if the emotional hook is sufficient. However, just engagement is not enough. The engaging activity must be tied to targeted standards and must be worth learning and spending time on.

Acquire new information and skills. Here, the new information and skills are presented and modeled. Students may acquire in a variety of ways, not always from teacher-directed "stand and deliver." Flexible grouping choices using the TAPS model may be considered here.

Apply new knowledge and skills. In this part of the lesson or chunk of the unit, the students apply their knowledge and skills to practice and gain proficiency. TAPS may be considered here also.

Assessment. Based on the standard or benchmark identified for the chunk or portion of the unit, this is how we will know that students have been successful in developing the required concept or skill.

CHUNKING THE LEARNING FOR SAMPLE UNIT PLANS

Let's take a look at how this template may be used to plan differentiated learning for the sample unit plans in Chapter 4. We can identify the variables we will be differentiating by using the adjustable learning elements discussed in Chapter 5.

The Weather Reporter, Grades K to 2

Having done an adjustable grid prior to the unit, we have some relevant data to begin planning this unit (see Figure 7.3). It helps us plan the depth of content and the response to our diverse learners. We may find, in some cases, that students are clustered in the "approaching mastery" and "high degree of mastery" columns depending on their previous experiences, or we may have a large group of learners who are only beginning with the concepts.

This primary unit has five chunks in its learning process:

1. Temperature and thermometers

2. The sun and heat-shade and sunny places

3. What do we need to do when the weather changes?

4. Reporting the weather

5. The seasons in our area and the weather

Figure 7.3 Adjustable Learning Grid: The Weather Reporter

	Standards-Based Content, Skill, or Assessment: Students know and understand interrelationships among science, technology, and human activity and how they can affect the world. Physical science: Weather and its impact **Pre-Assessment Tool or Method:** 1. Discuss these two questions with students and note responses. 2. Read a book about the seasons as a class and make predictions about the weather.		
B	Plan for daily living and activities based on weather	Extend their list of characteristics of the seasons	Need to be able to name the seasons and characteristics
	Can name and describe seasons	Predict impact of weather on daily living	Recognize the connections between weather and daily living
A	Correlate weather with activities and clothing needs Describe impact of seasons on daily living	List the seasons and some characteristics of each Correlate weather with activities and clothing needs	Describe personal physical reaction to weather "I had to put a jacket on" "I was so hot I was thirsty" When prompted could give a characteristic of a season
	High Degree	*Approaching*	*Beginning*

We will look at what might happen in a differentiated learning situation with Chunk 5, recognizing that there are many ways to get to the standards; there may be as many scenarios as there are creative teachers (Figure 7.4).

Figure 7.4 Planning for Differentiated Learning: The Weather Reporter

Planning for Differentiated Learning	
Unit Title: The Weather Reporter	***Grade Level:*** K to 2
Standards: What should students know and be able to do for this portion of the unit (chunk)? 5. The seasons in our area and the weather	***Pre-Assessment Lesson Strategy:*** Use the data from the adjustable grid designed from the unit pre-assessment tool to start the unit and data from formative assessments throughout the unit such as journals, ticket out, quick writes, quizzes
Critical Question for This Portion of the Unit: I. Can you tell what the weather will be like during the winter, spring, summer, and fall?	***Personal Question(s):*** Students will place a question about the season on a graffiti board so that they may have a personal commitment to the learning. (Differentiating Interest/Choice)
Content: (Concepts) Seasons Temperature	***Skills:*** (What will students do?) Standard/Benchmark 6: Students describe the type of weather characteristics for each season

Activate: (Creating focus and purpose) Small heterogeneous *concept formation* groups will be given an envelope containing pictures of various seasons depicting weather, clothing, scenes, and activities. Ask students to group pictures based on like attributes (Differentiating Process) Have groups report out on their groupings and their rationale for those groups (Some groups may actually organize by season whereas others may do so by clothing, activities, etc.)
Acquire: (Getting the information and grouping choices) ***Total Groups Discussion:*** Students remain with their groups ***Question Prompts:*** I.   If it were cold out what would people need to wear? (Students in their groups will select and hold up picture) 2.   What is something we could do in hot weather? 3.   What does winter look like?

(Continued)

Figure 7.4 (Continued)

---

4. What do people often do in spring?

5. Which season do you like best and why?

Invite students to go to one of the *four corners* of the room, each labeled with one of the seasons. There they will discuss with the other students who have selected that season why they chose that one and what they like about it. The students pair up with a partner and design a poster or statement to show why their season is the best.

Using large chart paper divided in four quadrants labeled with the four seasons, students are given a bank of vocabulary words (such as warm, hot, sunny, shady, heat, chilly, sticky, swimming, hiking, skating) as well as pictures from their envelope and place them in the appropriate quadrant. (Use tables or floor for working space) (Differentiating Communication/Technology) (Differentiating Multiple Intelligences)

Formative Assessment: (Demonstrating the learning)

In your season construction paper book, one season per page, draw and write the following in each of three sections. (Differentiating Interest/Choice)

I am dressed for _____ wearing my _____.

I like to _____ in _____ because _____.

My house looks like this in _____. It has _____.

Students will resource vocabulary and pictures from previous activities. Learners who are at a more proficient level of verbal ability may write without sentence stems. Less able writers may use inventive spelling and correct it for the final product.

Although we have only considered one chunk of the unit, there are ample opportunities to integrate best-practice instructional strategies in this or other chunks focusing on student thinking and standards. One way to differentiate in the final assessment might be to use a choice board (Figure 7.5) that allows students to select their own preferences but still achieves the targeted standards.

Figure 7.5 Choice Board: The Weather Reporter (Differentiating Content and Materials) (Differentiating Communication/Technology)

Prepare a CNN report on the computer; use pictures and words	Draw a storyboard with captions to share your weather report	Prepare a television weather report and deliver it
Create a song to report the weather	Wild Card! You choose	Prepare a PowerPoint to share your weather report
Make a play about your weather report	Make a weather board and use it to report the weather	Write a poem about the weather

"The Survey Says . . . ," Grades 3 to 5

In this unit, the pre-assessment serves to gather data about student skills in relationship to data analysis. It also serves as a preview of the unit to come. Creating the adjustable grid (Figure 7.6) helps us plot that data and gives us information about the class as a whole as well as individual student needs. The grid records degree of competency, not the number of students in each column.

The chunks for this unit are as follows:

1. Activating learning for the total unit and developing a survey question

2. Learning about visual representations of data

3. Summarizing using median and mean

4. Predicting with data

5. Analyzing data results and sharing

Figure 7.6   Adjustable Learning Grid: "The Survey Says . . . "

Standards-Based Content, Skill, or Assessment: Grade 3 to 5 Mathematics		
Data Analysis and Probability: Develop and evaluate inferences and predictions that are based on data		
Pre-Assessment Tool or Method:		
Have students examine a variety of graphs and charts and predict and interpret data. Quick write (topic sentence and supporting detail and rationale)		
B Require complex data and challenging predictions that are relevant to their lives	Opportunities to collect, organize, and predict from data in a variety of situations	Beginning with simple data collection Provide a variety of ways to organize data Practice in making simple predictions
A Quite capable of interpreting data and also organizing and recording in a variety of forms Understands averages Can analyze and summarize data to make predictions	Is able to understand and interpret data Can organize simple data in limited ways Limited predictions can be made from data	Has little experience with understanding and interpreting data Not able to define median and mean
High Degree	*Approaching*	*Beginning*

If we use Chunk 1, Figure 7.7 shows what the sample planning grid could look like.

Figure 7.7   Planning for Differentiated Learning: "The Survey Says . . ."

Planning for Differentiated Learning	
Unit Title: The Survey Says . . .	**Grade Level:** Math 3 to 5
Standards: What should students know and be able to do for this portion of the unit (chunk)? Activating learning for the total unit and developing a survey question	**Pre-Assessment Lesson Strategy:** Use the data from the adjustable grid designed from unit pre-assessment tool to start the unit and data from formative assessments throughout the unit such as journals, ticket out, quick writes, quizzes
Critical Question for This Portion of the Unit: How can we use data to predict how people think about and choose preferences?	**Personal Question(s):** Generated by students after activating the learning
Content: (Concepts) Data Investigate Predict	**Skills:** (What will students do?) Benchmark 1: Students will design investigations to address a question

Activate: (Creating focus and purpose)

Class will engage in the mock game based on television show *Family Feud*

Students will work in *triads* and be given a survey questions to ask of other students. They will collect the answers from students in the classroom and display the responses. Then they will rank the top three responses. The teacher sets up the game that will use these survey results. Two teams of students will compete. All students will get a chance to be on a team.

The *whole class* develops three criteria for good survey questions.

Teacher shares critical question for this unit and asks students to *personalize* it in their math journal.

Acquire: (Getting the information and grouping choices)

Total group: Rationale for need to analyze data and survey. Real-world examples of how surveys are used. *Direct instruction* on how to design a survey, ways to collect data, tally, and present a variety of ways to organize data (*pie chart, vertical bar graph,* etc.). Independent application or representation of simple data presented. (Differentiating Process)

Alone: Write a survey question (Differentiating Interest/Choice) ***Partner work:*** Structured by teacher to peer-edit their survey questions based on criteria identified	
Formative Assessment: (Demonstrating the learning) Using an *inside-outside circle*, students will present and test their edited survey questions (Differentiating Multiple Intelligences)	

Do You Know Your Rights? Grades 5 to 8

Figure 7.8 shows the adjustable learning grid for this unit on the Bill of Rights. Constructed from the pre-assessment data, this adjustable grid shows us what students know and are able to do at the beginning of the unit. As before, the grid does not show the number of students in each column but their degree of competency.

Figure 7.8   Adjustable Learning Grid: Do You Know Your Rights?

	Impact	Historical foundation	What is it?
B		Current personal tie	Learn basic elements of the Bill How might it help us today?
A	Knowledgeable about the Declaration of Independence, Constitution, and the Bill of Rights and their impact	Know some aspects of the Bill but not its significance	Students are aware of the term *Bill of Rights* but not its impact or content
	High Degree	*Approaching*	*Beginning*

Standards-Based Content, Skill, or Assessment: Grades 5 to 8

Students are able to describe the basic ideas set forth in the Declaration of Independence, Constitution, and Bill of Rights

Pre-Assessment Tool or Method:

A Ticket Out can be filled in by students, asking them to explain their understanding of the Bill of Rights

For this lesson plan, we will focus on student learning for Chunks 1 and 2 (see Figure 7.9).

1. Activating the unit through relevance and application to students' lives

2. Developing a sense of historical background and context, including the concepts of freedom and citizenship; for example, What were some of the influences that led to the Preamble and the first ten amendments?

Figure 7.9   Planning for Differentiated Learning: Do You Know Your Rights?

Planning for Differentiated Learning	
Unit Title: Do You Know Your Rights?	***Grade Level:*** 5 to 8
Standards: What should students know and be able to do for this portion of the unit (chunk)? 1. Activate the unit through relevance and application to students' lives 2. Develop a sense of historical background and context, including the concepts of freedom and citizenship. What were some of the influences that led to the Preamble and the first ten rights?	***Pre-Assessment Lesson Strategy:*** Use the data from the adjustable grid designed from unit pre-assessment tool to start the unit and data from formative assessments throughout the unit such as journals, ticket out, quick writes, quizzes
Critical Question for This Portion of the Unit: 1. How will you compare the reasons the Bill of Rights was drafted and the reasons it is still a powerful and influential document today?	***Personal Question(s):*** Generated by students after activating the learning
Content: (Concepts) Bill of Rights Constitution Historical context	***Skills:*** (What will students do?) Benchmark a: (as in curriculum unit plan) Students will explain the reasons for the Bill of Rights and how this critical document has changed over time

Activate: (Creating focus and purpose)

One way for a teacher to set the stage for this unit is to bring in the following:

- A school district job application or college application with a nondiscrimination clause
- A copy of the Miranda rights (from the local police)
- A copy of a blank tax form
- A newspaper
- A ballot
- A church bulletin or notice

Students are given a summary copy of the Bill of Rights and organized into *small heterogeneous groups.* Ask students from each group to explain to the whole group which right corresponds to a particular document. In addition, ask if they can think of any other examples.

Acquire: (Getting the information and grouping choices)

Total group:

Before viewing: Divide into groups of five. Give each group a five-section puzzle or star with five questions on it. Each student will use a point of a puzzle or star with their question. The Bill of Rights is the central idea.

1. Why were the amendments written?
2. List some of the issues that led to the Bill of Rights
3. Did everyone agree? Why or why not?
4. What else was going on in the colonies at that time?
5. What were some of the influences that led to the Preamble?

Students will take notes on their questions during the video. *(Jigsaw strategy)* (Special needs or English as a second language learners may work with a partner)

Total group: View video clip from PBS on *Creation of the Bill of Rights* and answer questions
Small groups: In a group of five, share answers to their question with the others and take notes on a summarizing star sheet. (See Figure 7.10)

Total group: Discussion to summarize historical context of Bill of Rights
Given the reasons for certain rights, are they still applicable today?
Which one is most important to you and why? *Think, Pair, Share*

Formative Assessment: (Demonstrating the learning)

Using a T chart: In the film, list some issues we still deal with today. On the right side, what are some issues that may be different today?

Resources: Film Notes and current newspaper or news magazine. Could be assigned as homework.

Same Issues	Different Issues

Students working in small groups may have a particular area of interest and may want to construct questions of their own concerning different amendments (Differentiating Interest/Choice) (see Figure 7.10).

We can also use tiering (Tomlinson, 2001) to challenge students at their readiness level in terms of depth of knowledge and ability to think abstractly, which means we will adjust the degree of complexity in the assignment for students at the various levels (Differentiating Readiness).

Figure 7.11 provides a set of tiered assignments for students at various levels of readiness. All are engaging and challenging assignments but at different levels of complexity.

Figure 7.10 Note-Taking Sheet: Do You Know Your Rights?

Persuasive Writing—Convince Me! Grades 9 to 12

In this unit of study, we have nine chunks:

1. Introducing persuasive writing: Why do we need it? How is it relevant?

2. Reviewing the model and rubric

3. Learning the pieces of good persuasive writing and practicing them

Figure 7.11 Tiered Assignments: Do You Know Your Rights?

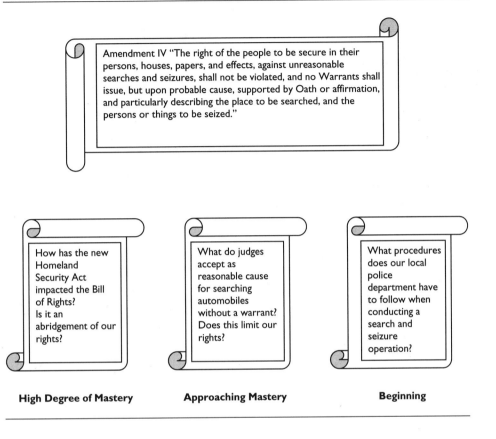

4. Writing compelling introductions and conclusions and adding background

5. Using evidence for and against a claim

6. Writing occasion and/or position statements to convey point of view

7. Varying voice, sentence style, and word choice to help the reader

8. Choosing an issue and researching point of view

9. Summarizing research and using a graphic organizer

Figure 7.12 details the learning for Chunks 8 and 9, and Figure 7.13 offers a Four-Corners Graphic Organizer for summarizing and note taking. Students also can use a self-evaluation checklist, like the following:

Figure 7.12   Planning for Differentiated Learning: Persuasive Writing—Convince Me!

Planning for Differentiated Learning	
Unit Title: Persuasive Writing—Convince Me!	**Grade Level:** 9 to 12
Standards: What should students know and be able to do for this portion of the unit (chunk)? Choosing an issue and researching your point of view	**Pre-Assessment Lesson Strategy:** Use the data from the adjustable grid designed from unit pre-assessment tool to start the unit and data from formative assessments throughout the unit such as journals, ticket out, quick writes, quizzes
Critical Question for This Portion of the Unit: 1. How can I research and write to persuade others that I have a valid point of view?	**Personal Question(s):** Information on research skills from previous unit
Content: (Concepts) Claim or position Rationale Voice	**Skills:** (What will students do?) *Standard 2:* 2. Students will choose and research evidence about a point of view on a controversial issue

Activate: (Creating focus and purpose)

Teacher asks students to do a *Quick Write* as a ticket out. They must persuade the teacher not to assign homework the next day. Teacher uses this as pre-assessment data to identify if the student can use the attributes of persuasive writing taught in the pervious chunk of the unit (vocabulary, voice, logic).

Acquire: (Getting the information and grouping choices)

Small groups: Students work in heterogeneous small groups of three to examine a few paragraphs of a highly persuasive speaker and analyze the attributes of compelling writing. Use the unit rubric considering voice and claim to assess the effectiveness. (e.g., Martin Luther King, John F. Kennedy, Rosa Parks) (Differentiating Content and Materials)

Total group: Class discussion about a hot issue in the school community. With a *random partner*, brainstorm possible topics and possible sources of information. Use a *four-corner placemat* for recording information and research. (Differentiating Process)

Alone: Write a well-constructed occasion/position (claim)

Clock partners: Using the rubric, be a critical friend to your partner's work (Differentiating Multiple Intelligences)

Formative Assessment: (Demonstrating the learning)

Using your placemat and your claim, produce a graphic organizer (Figure 7.13) on your point of view on the hot issue in our school. (Differentiating Interest/Choice) This will help students practice using the organizer that goes with the final assessment. Use a self-evaluation checklist and set a personal goal (Figure 7.14). (Differentiating Multiple Intelligences)

Figure 7.13 Four-Corners Graphic Organizer for Summarizing and Note Taking:
The Hot Issues

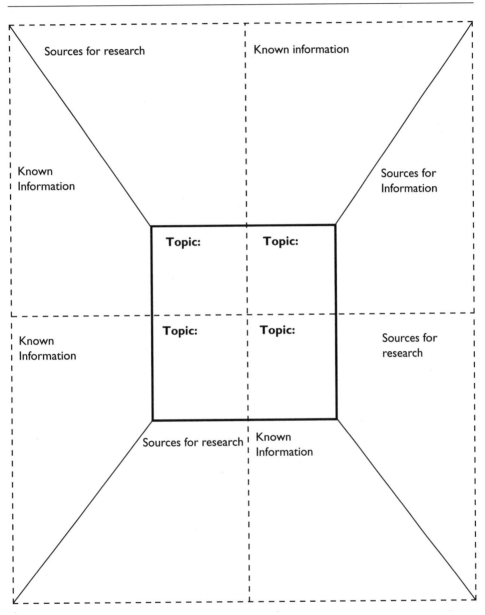

Self-Evaluation Checklist for Persuasive Writing

Students will respond to each statement with one of the following: Yes, Somewhat, Not really

_____ Claim indicates why this issue is important to student.

_____ Claim is well supported by the reasons for and reasons against other points of view.

_____ Writing has a clear introduction and a logical conclusion that are supported by evidence.

_____ Word choice is varied and suited to the theme.

_____ Writing is clearly geared to a specific audience or reader.

_____ Sentences are varied in length and type to add interest to the letter.

_____ Writing is edited and submitted error-free.

_____ Primary and secondary sources are used and quoted appropriately.

Based on how students answered their checklists, they can set personal goals for improvement.

SUMMARY

We hope these samples show you why the data are needed and how to put them together to make meaningful decisions about differentiated learning experiences for diverse learners. By using these data driven methods, we can keep our planning tied to the required standards and assessments for high-stakes learning.

Differentiation comes in many forms. The thoughtful practitioner recognizes that one size doesn't fit all and that it takes careful planning and ongoing assessment to reach all students and ensure their continuing growth, achievement, and success.

 # Conclusion

Putting It All Together for Student Growth and Achievement

HOW DO WE DO ALL THIS WITHOUT RUNNING FROM THE ROOM SCREAMING?

During a recent discussion about the climate in his building, a new principal posed an interesting question. He had observed that teachers were uncertain about how they were doing on several new initiatives, and the principal himself was in doubt about how to address their uncertainty because that kind of discussion interfered with progress on the initiatives.

We began to discuss the feedback loop and process in his supervision practice. The astute principal concluded that the unrest he had heard in teachers' voices and a reduction in their risk taking were alerting him to a change in building climate. Together, we developed a plan to adjust the feedback frequency, consistency, and content in his practice. Checking back a few weeks later, we found that the principal was beginning to note a more positive shift in the school climate. This principal then had to grapple with several new and challenging questions: What aspects of feedback are most valuable? How do we know whether there is a problem? What solutions might bring about desired results and with which staff members?

By addressing issues of adult learning and change in the areas of school climate and culture, we can create a supportive environment for meeting diverse student needs. At a time when high-stakes state assessments are adding to the anxiety level and remain a focus for everything from scheduling to resource allocation, it is important to remember that we need to give each other feedback and opportunities for celebration at regular intervals. Without ongoing dialogue among teachers and educational leaders, major changes will get stalled.

We need to take one step at a time. When it comes to using data to make good decisions about differentiation, there is no magic formula. We can enter the stream through a variety of channels. Some schools or teachers may wish to start with assessment. Others may want to try an adjustable assignment first to see how it works. Still others will start by addressing the climate and learning style of students (and hopefully of teachers too). *Enter at any point, limit your focus, and spend time dialoguing about what works and for which students.*

WHAT CAN WE LEARN FROM THE ERRORS AND SUCCESSES OF THE BEST TEACHERS?

A veteran teacher leaned over at a recent meeting and disclosed that in the last five years, she had learned more about teaching and learning than in the previous twenty-five years combined. This incredible teacher was so excited and passionate about student success that she told everyone she knew about how much better teaching was in today's classrooms. Lifelong learning and celebration are always themes among top-notch teachers. The best teachers simply sound different from all the rest.

Incredible teachers look for underlying causes that they can control. They empower students to be a part of the learning process. Their classrooms feel different, with energy levels and success rates that have textures of their own. The best teachers share with colleagues and value the dialogue and time needed to help each other hone their craft.

A recent school visit for a book study about differentiated instruction (Gregory, 2003) was an illustration of differences. Teachers who felt empowered by the new learning were sharing how the beginning use of new strategies was going in their classrooms. Some of the really excellent teachers shared errors they had made and how they knew when there were problems that needed to be solved. They shared possible solutions and invited others to help them develop more and better ideas for correcting the problems. This conversation took place at 4:30 P.M. after a long day of instruction. However, the teachers were still enthusiastic learners and willing to help each other risk and share. The clincher came when the principal modeled risk-taking behavior and described some of the things he was excited about in the classroom. The best teachers influence all aspects of a school's climate and action level. Positive, reflective adult learning is catching.

Teachers who frequently feel overwhelmed, who have a sense of a full plate that keeps getting fuller all the time, may need to learn from expert teachers who have tamed some of these feelings. The best teachers focus on fewer things, including standards and techniques. They figure out what really matters, what they can and cannot control or influence, and then they carefully select a course of action given the data they have collected. We can reduce the stress of new initiatives by looking at what effective teachers do to manage the load (Reeves, 2003).

We suggest the same for you as you use the tools and techniques described in this book. It is important to focus on one aspect of the learner as you collect data. Then select a manageable technique or set of techniques that may work to meet diverse needs. Be certain to build in time to share with others, because this is not a journey you should take by yourself. *Dialogue, ask questions, and reflect on what you learn. And then model those steps for your students.*

WHY IS IT ALWAYS ABOUT THE STUDENT?

In a standards-based, high-stakes climate, teaching and learning have to be about the student and the teacher's support of the students. We have spent many years trying to focus on teacher actions and verbalizations in classrooms. We have just begun to spend time focusing on what students are doing, saying, using, and demonstrating as they interact or perform. When we listen and question carefully, we can use what we know about learning and learners to more accurately plan instruction and learning opportunities.

Differentiation is a personal philosophy that helps us constantly consider the multitude of choices that are available for learning. Differentiation helps us identify and understand

- The variety of pathways leading to targeted standards
- Where each student is in regard to the standards
- What we know about each student's learning profile, interests, and readiness for learning tasks

When we clearly know our learners, we can make informed choices and adjust the learning processes so that all students have an optimal chance of succeeding.

That is what it is about: *all students growing and achieving as fast and as far as they can, with the right kind of coaching from their teachers, who are responding to the data available about student learning at any and every given point in time.*

References

Ainsworth, Larry. (2003a). *Power standards: Identifying the standards that matter the most.* Denver, CO: Advanced Learning Press and Center for Performance Assessment.

Ainsworth, Larry. (2003b). *Unwrapping the standards: A simple process to make standards manageable.* Denver, CO: Advanced Learning Press and Center for Performance Assessment.

Aronson, E. (1978). *The jigsaw classroom.* Beverly Hills, CA: Sage.

Ausubel, D. P. (1960). The use of advance organizers in the learning and retention of meaningful verbal material. *Journal of Educational Psychology, 51,* 267–272.

Bellanca, J., & Fogarty, R. (1991). *Blueprints for thinking in the cooperative classroom* (2nd ed.). Arlington Heights, IL: Skylight.

Bennett, W. J. (1986). *What works: Research about teaching and learning.* Washington, DC: U.S. Department of Education.

Bloom, B., et al. (1985). *Taxonomy of educational objectives handbook 1: Cognitive domain.* New York: David McKay.

Brophy, J. E. (1996). *Teaching problem students.* New York: Guilford.

Bruner, J. (1966). *Toward a theory of instruction.* Cambridge, MA: Harvard University Press.

Burns, Timothy. (1996). *From risk to resilience: A journey with heart for our children, our future.* Dallas, TX: The Marco Polo Group.

Buzan, T. (1974). *Use both sides of your brain.* New York: Dutton.

Caine, Renate, & Caine, Geoffrey. (1991). *Making connections: Teaching and human brain.* New York: Addison-Wesley.

Caine, Renate, & Caine, Geoffrey. (1997). *Education on the edge of possibility.* Alexandria, VA: Association for Supervision and Curriculum Development (ASCD).

Caswell, H. L., & Campbell, D. S. (1935). *Curriculum development.* New York: American Book Company.

Cawelti, G. (Ed.). (1995). *Handbook of research on improving student achievement.* Arlington, VA: Educational Research Service.

Conner, Daryl. (1993). *Managing at the speed of change.* New York: Villard Books.

Costa, Arthur. (1991). *The school as a home for the mind.* Arlington Heights, IL: Skylight.

Costa, Arthur, & Garmston, Robert. (1994). *The art of cognitive coaching.* Norwood, MA: Christopher Gordon.

Creemers, P. B. M. (1994). *The effective classroom.* London: Cassell.

Csikszentmihalyi, M. (1990). *Flow: The psychology of optimal experience.* New York: Harper Perennial.

Cunningham, Dorothy. (1999). *Preschool curriculum: A child-centered curriculum of concepts and activities including all of the CDA functional areas.* Washington, DC: ERIC.

Damasio, A. (1999). *The feeling of what happens: Body and emotion in the making of consciousness.* New York: Harcourt Brace.

Deal, Terrence E., & Peterson, Kent D. (1998). *Shaping school culture: The heart leadership.* San Francisco: Jossey-Bass.

De Bono, Edward. (1987). *Edward de Bono's cort thinking.* Boston: Advanced Practical Thinking.

Depree, Max. (1989). *Leadership is an art.* New York: Doubleday.

Doyle, W. (1986). Classroom organization and management. In M. C. Wittrock (Ed.), *Handbook of research on teaching* (3rd ed., pp. 392–431). New York: Macmillan.

Duke, D. L. (1979). Editor's preface. In D. L. Duke (Ed.), *Classroom management* (78th Yearbook of the National Society for the Study of Education, Part 2, pp. i–xxi). Chicago: University of Chicago Press.

Dunn, Rita, (1990, Winter). Teaching underachievers through their learning style strengths. *International Education, 16*(52), 5–7.

Elder, Linda, & Paul, Richard. (2002). *The art of asking essential questions.* San Francisco: Foundation for Critical Thinking.

Fogarty, Robin, & Bellanca, Jim. (1993). *Patterns for thinking, patterns for transfer: A cooperative team approach for critical and creative thinking in the classroom.* Arlington Heights, IL: IRI/Skylight.

Gardner, Howard. (1983). *Frames of mind: The theory of multiple intelligences.* New York: Basic Books.

Gardner, Howard. (1993). *Multiple intelligences: The theory in practice.* New York: Basic Books.

Given, Barbara K. (2002). *Teaching to the brain's natural learning systems.* Alexandria, VA: ASCD.

Gordon, W. (1961). *Synectics.* New York: Harper & Row.

Gregorc, Anthony. (1982). *Inside styles: Beyond the basics.* Connecticut: Gregorc Associates.

Gregory, Gayle. (2003). *Differentiated instructional strategies in practice: Training, implementation, and supervision.* Thousand Oaks, CA: Corwin Press.

Gregory, Gayle, & Chapman, Carolyn. (2002). *Differentiated instructional strategies: One size doesn't fit all.* Thousand Oaks, CA: Corwin Press.

Harris, J. R. (1998). *The nurture assumption.* New York: Free Press.

Hart, Leslie. (1993). *Human brain and human learning.* Arizona: Books for Education.

Hattie, J. A. (1992). Measuring the effects of schooling. *Australian Journal of Education, 36*(1), 5–13.

Healy, Jane. (1990). *Endangered minds: Why our children don't think.* New York: Simon & Schuster.

Hill, S., & Hancock, J. (1993). *Reading and writing communities.* Armadale, Australia: Eleanor Curtin.

Jacobs, Heidi Hayes. (1997). *Mapping the big picture: Integrating curriculum and assessment K–12.* Alexandria, VA: ASCD.

Johnson, David, & Johnson, Roger. (1991). *Cooperative learning lesson structures.* Edina, MN: Interaction Books.

Johnson, David, & Johnson, Roger. (1998). *Learning together and alone* (5th ed.). Boston: Allyn & Bacon.

Kagan, Spencer. (1994). *Cooperative learning.* San Clemente, CA: Kagan Publications.

Kantor, Rosabeth M. (1985). Why people resist change. *Management Review.*

Kessler, Rachael. (2000). *The soul of education: Helping students find connection, compassion, and character at school.* Alexandria, VA: ASCD.

Kohn, Alfie. (2002). *The schools our children deserve: Moving beyond traditional classrooms and "tougher standards."* New York: Mariner Books.

Kolb, David. (1984). *Experiential learning: Experience as the source of learning and development.* Englewood Cliffs, NJ: Prentice Hall.

Kuzmich, Lin. (1998). *Data driven instruction: A handbook.* Longmont, CO: Centennial Board of Cooperative Services.

Kuzmich, Lin. (2002). *Scenario-based learning.* Paper presented to New Orleans Archdiocese administrators.

Levine, M. (2002). *A mind at a time.* New York: Simon & Schuster.

Lou, Y., Abrami, P. C., Spence, J. C., Paulsen, C., Chamber, B., & d'Apollonio, S. (1996). Within-class grouping: A meta-analysis. *Journal of Educational Research, 75,* 69–77.

Marzano, Robert. (2003). *What works in schools: Translating research into action.* Alexandria, VA: ASCD.

Marzano, Robert, Pickering, D. J., & Pollack, J. E. (2001). *Classroom instruction that works.* Alexandria, VA: ASCD.

McCarthy, Bernice. (1990). Using the 4MAT system to bring learning styles to schools. *Educational Leadership, 48*(2), 31–37.

McCombs, Barbara, & Whisler, Jo Sue. (1997). *The learner-centered classroom and school: Strategies for increasing student motivation and achievement.* San Francisco: Jossey-Bass.

McNeely, Clea, Nonnemaker, James, & Blum, Robert. (2002). Promoting school connectedness: Evidence from the National Longitudinal Study of Adolescent Heath. *The Journal of School Health, 72*(4), 138–146.

Milgram, R., Dunn, R., & Price, G. (1993). *Teaching and counseling gifted and talented adolescents.* Westport, CT: Praeger.

Nagy, William. (2000). *Teaching vocabulary to improve reading comprehension.* Washington, DC: ERIC.

Ogle, D. (1986). K-W-L: A teaching model that develops active reading of expository text. *Reading Teacher,* pp. 564–574.

Olivia, P. F. (1982). *Developing the curriculum.* Boston: Little Brown.

Orlich, Donald, Harder, Robert, Callahan, Richard, Kravas, Constance, Kauchak, Donald, Pendergrass, R. A., Keogh, Andre, & Hellene, Dorothy. (1980). *Teaching strategies: A guide to better instruction.* Lexington, MA: D. C. Heath.

Ornstein, R. (1986). *Multimind: A new way of looking at human behavior.* New York: Doubleday.

Palmer, P. (1993). *To know as we are known.* San Francisco: Harper San Francisco.

Panksepp, J. (1998). *Affective neuroscience.* New York: Oxford University Press.

Parry, Terence, & Gregory, Gayle. (2003). *Designing brain compatible learning.* Arlington Heights, IL: Skylight.

Paul, Richard, & Elder, Linda. (2001). *Critical thinking: Tools for taking charge of your learning and your life.* New Jersey: Prentice Hall.

Perkins, D. (1995). *Outsmarting IQ.* New York: Free Press.

Pert, C. (1993). The chemical communicators. In B. Moyers (Ed.), *Healing and the mind* (pp. 177–193). New York: Doubleday.

Reeves, Douglas B. (2000). *Accountability in action: A blueprint for learning organizations.* Denver, CO: Advanced Learning Press and Center for Performance Assessment.

Reeves, Douglas B. (2003). *The daily disciplines of leadership.* Denver, CO: Advanced Learning Press and Center for Performance Assessment.

Restak, R. (1994). *The modular brain.* New York: Vintage.

Rickard, Patricia, & Stiles, Richard. (1985). Comprehensive adult student assessment system design for effective assessment in correctional educational programs. *Journal of Correctional Education, 36*(2), 51–53.

Roeber, Edward. (1996). *Guidelines for the development and management of performance assessments.* Washington, DC: ERIC Clearinghouse on Assessment and Evaluation.

Rozman, Deborah. (1998, March). Speech at Symposium on the Brain, University of California, Berkeley.

Saylor, J. G., & Alexander, W. M. (1974). *Planning curriculum for schools.* New York: Holt, Rinehart & Winston.

Silver, Harvey, Strong, Richard, & Perini, Matthew. (2000). *So each may learn: Integrating learning styles and multiple intelligences.* Alexandria, VA: ASCD.

Slavin, R. E. (1986). *Using student team learning.* Baltimore, MD: Center for Research on Elementary and Middle Schools, Johns Hopkins University.

Sternberg, Robert. (1996). *Successful intelligence.* New York: Simon & Schuster.

Stiggins, R. (1993, May 5). *Authentic assessment.* Workshop presented at the "Train the Trainers" conference in Toronto, Canada.

Stiggins, Richard J. (1997). *Student-centered classroom assessment* (2nd ed.). Columbus, OH: Merrill, an imprint of Prentice Hall.

Stigler, James W., & Hiebert, James. (1999). *The teaching gap: Best ideas from the world's teachers for improving education in the classroom.* New York: Free Press.

Taba, H. (1967). *Teachers' handbook for elementary social studies.* Reading, MA: Addison Wesley.

Thornburg, David. (2002). *The new basics education and the future of work in the telematic age.* Alexandria, VA: ASCD

Tomlinson, Carol Ann. (2001). *How to differentiate instruction in the mixed-ability classroom* (2nd ed.). Alexandria, VA: ASCD.

Torrance, Paul E. (1995). *Why fly? A philosophy of creativity.* Norwood, NJ: Ablex.

Vail, Priscilla. (1989). *Smart kids with school problems.* New York: New American Library.

Wang, M. C., Haertel, G. D., & Walberg, H. J. (1993). Toward a knowledge base for school learning. *Review of Educational Research, 63*(3), 249–294.

Wasley, P., Hampel, R., & Clark, R. (1997). *Kids and school reform.* San Francisco: Jossey-Bass.

Wiggins, Grant, & McTighe, Jay. (1998). *Understanding by design.* Alexandria, VA: ASCD.

Williams, Julian, & Ryan, Julie. (2000). National testing and the improvement of classroom teacher: Can they coexist? *British Educational Research Journal, 26*(1), 49–74.

Wright, R. (1994). *The moral animal.* New York: Vintage.

Index

**CORWIN
PRESS**

The Corwin Press logo—a raven striding across an open book—represents the union of courage and learning. Corwin Press is committed to improving education for all learners by publishing books and other professional development resources for those serving the field of K–12 education. By providing practical, hands-on materials, Corwin Press continues to carry out the promise of its motto: **"Helping Educators Do Their Work Better."**